ULTIMATE
CHRISTMAS

ULTIMATE
CHRISTMAS

Love Food® is an imprint of Parragon Books Ltd

Parragon
Queen Street House
4 Queen Street
Bath BA1 1HE, UK

ISBN: 978-1-4075-4383-3
Printed in China

Produced by the Bridgewater Book Company Ltd
Cover design by Talking Design
Craft projects created and written by Emma Frith
New recipes written by Sarah Banbery
Introduction written by Sara Harper
Craft projects photography by Andrew Perris
Craft projects styled by Isabel de Cordova
New recipe photography by Laurie Evans
Home economy by Carol Tennant
Additional photography by Mark Wood

The publisher would like to thank the following for permission to reproduce copyright material: Bettmann/Corbis: 4; Dorling Kindersley/Getty Images: 10 (top); Photonica/Getty Images: 10 (bottom); Mike Bentley/iStockphoto: 11; Sergej Petrakov/iStockphoto: 12; Lisa Thornberg/iStockphoto: 13; The Image Bank/Getty Images: 14; Iconica/Getty Images: 16; Jupiter Images: 17; StockFood/Getty Images: 21; and Malte Danielsson/Etsa/Corbis: 25.

Notes for the Reader

This book uses imperial, metric, or US cup measurements. Follow the same units of measurement throughout; do not mix imperial and metric. All spoon measurements are level: teaspoons are assumed to be 5 ml, and tablespoons are assumed to be 15 ml. Unless otherwise stated, milk is assumed to be whole, eggs and individual vegetables such as potatoes are medium, and pepper is freshly ground black pepper. Recipes using raw or very lightly cooked eggs should be avoided by infants, the elderly, pregnant women, convalescents, and anyone suffering from an illness. The times given are an approximate guide only.

Contents

Introduction

Christmas is the time to make your home warm and welcoming, festoon it with festive decorations, and infuse it with the aroma of enticing foods made from favorite recipes handed down over the years. It's a time of goodwill and giving, for celebrating with family and close friends. For some people, the religious aspect of Christmas has all but disappeared, but there's still a good underlying reason to celebrate. It's not about spending vast amounts of money in an effort to outdo and impress; it's about having a good time with people you care about. This is the perfect guide for creating a memorable Christmas at home, with fresh and inspiring ideas for making the most of the festive season.

In this book, you'll find out why we celebrate Christmas and where most of our traditions come from. There are even suggestions to help you establish your own customs,

to make Christmas even more special for you. To reduce the stress of the Christmas season, there's a section on getting organized, with a Christmas diary, handy tips on choosing a good Christmas tree, and suggestions for organizing a party and how to entertain your guests.

You will also find a selection of craft projects for you and your family to undertake, including ideas for making beautiful cards and simple decorations for your home.

COOKING AT CHRISTMAS

Whether your Christmas dinner is a huge family feast or a quiet dinner for one or two, you'll find plenty of recipe ideas to suit every occasion. This book features a tempting blend of favorite traditional recipes and updated classics with a contemporary twist, so you can keep up with family traditions and create some new ones of your own. Easy yet impressive recipes will inspire you to make fabulous food for friends

and family throughout the vacation, with irresistible options to satisfy meat-eaters and vegetarians alike. There's advice on planning your Christmas feast and suggestions for managing your Christmas cooking, enabling you to get the preparations under control and giving you the chance to relax and enjoy the day with your friends and family. Finally, there are helpful tips on turkeys and also ideas for decorating your table.

You don't need a mind-boggling array of kitchen equipment, nor do you need to be a culinary genius to create these mouthwatering meals. The recipes are clear and easy to follow, with gorgeous full-color photography throughout to enable you to produce fabulous food effortlessly, every time. The recipes have been devised with an underlying understanding of which ingredients work together in the pan and on the plate for spectacular results, and the ingredients are seasonal and readily sourced.

CHAPTER 1

All About
Chris

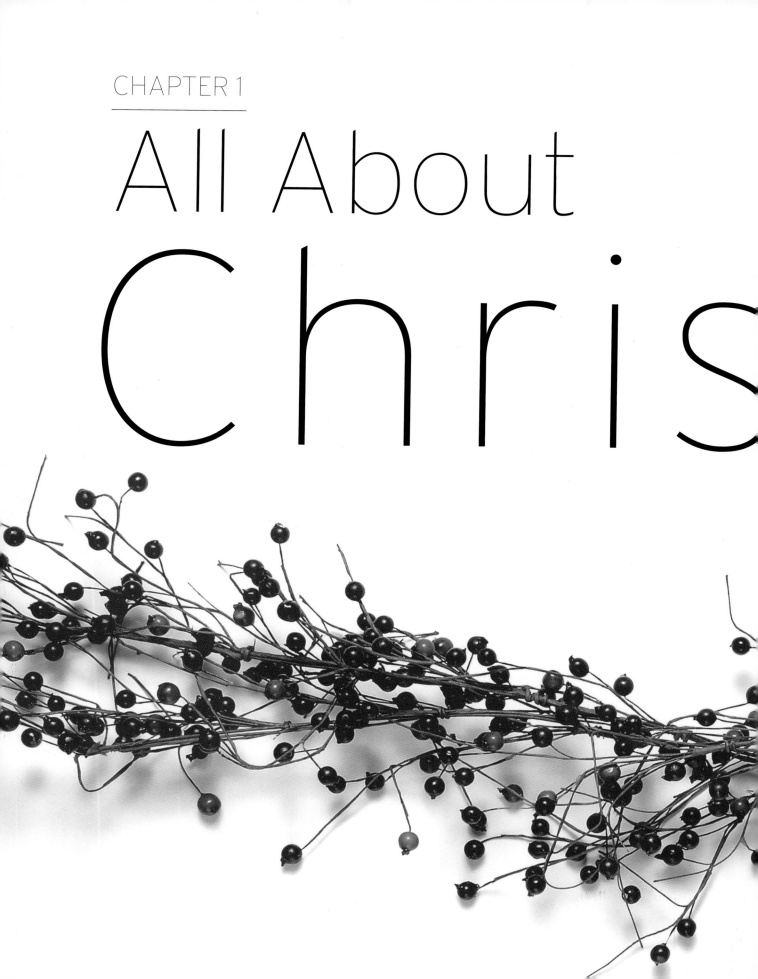

tmas

Christmas is an important occasion in the year because it's a time when we get together with family and friends. The following pages explain why we celebrate Christmas, and also give an insight into the many traditions that have arisen over the years. There is also a practical guide on how to organize and prepare for the vacation well in advance.

What is *Christmas?*

Christmas is a celebration of the birth of Christ, although no-one knows the day when he was actually born. Today, it's a major vacation and holy day, and even those who are not religious observe this festival as a special time to spend with families and friends.

The practice of celebrating the 25th day of December as Christ's birthday originates from the 4th century (before this time it had been a movable feast), and the choice of this particular day was probably influenced by pagan festivals held at that time in Europe. During the 6th century, the tradition of the twelve-day holy festival was established, starting on Christmas Day and ending on the morning of the Epiphany (January 6). The Epiphany either marks the arrival of the three wise men or the magi bearing gifts, or Christ's baptism, depending on which particular type of Christianity people follow.

The popularity of Christmas grew until the Reformation in Europe in the 16th century, a time of widespread religious upheaval that caused many Christians to stop celebrating Christmas because it included so many pagan customs. In many countries, Christmas festivities didn't become that important again until the 19th century, when St Nicholas was transformed into Santa Claus, changing the spirit of Christmas into what we recognize today. One large organization that's played a big part in helping to shape our perceptions of what Christmas entails is Macy's Department Store in New York. It scored a number of memorable firsts in the 19th century: the first to have late-night Christmas shopping, the first to have festive window displays, and the first to have a resident Santa Claus.

HOW CHRISTMAS IS CELEBRATED TODAY

The celebration of Christmas is the most popular religious-based public festival in the world, and its arrival in December is often prepared for months in advance by some people. During the Christmas season, people decorate their homes, city streets sparkle with colored lights, and the sound of Christmas music, both traditional carols and more modern popular songs, fills the air. Many department stores hire people to dress up as Santa Claus and listen to children's requests for gifts. People share festive greetings by sending Christmas cards to relatives and friends. On Christmas Eve, children hang up stockings for Santa Claus to fill with gifts, and many people go to a carol concert in their local church. Christmas Day usually culminates in the unwrapping of presents and a fabulous feast.

How to survive & enjoy the Christmas season

There's a saying that at Christmas-time it's a race to see which will give out first—your feet or your wallet. To make your Christmas more pleasurable, follow these top tips:

- ★ Try to avoid being too ambitious when you are choosing presents (this will help your bank balance as well).
- ★ Many stores let you order online, minimizing time spent in crowded stores.
- ★ Scale down your ambitions. If you're a working parent, you'll wear yourself ragged if you feel obliged to do everything yourself, from baking to cardmaking. Choose one thing that you really enjoy doing to make Christmas special (such as making cookies with your children), and save the rest for years when you're not so short of time.
- ★ Establish your own traditions instead of doing what everyone else does.
- ★ Avoid family conflicts and call a truce on unresolved problems.
- ★ Share the workload—invite your guests to bring canapés or desserts to your party instead of trying to do all the cooking and baking yourself.
- ★ Give yourself a break. Finding time for yourself may seem almost impossible at this time of year, but if you do, you're more likely to relax. And if you're relaxed, your family and friends are more likely to enjoy themselves.

Christmas
Traditions

There are numerous traditions that are associated with Christmas, from giving gifts and cards to one another and decorating a tree, to hanging a wreath on the door, and kissing under the mistletoe, but do you know where some of these traditions originated from?

The Christmas season is steeped in familiar, old traditions. Decorating our homes, trimming the tree, and exchanging gifts are staples of the season. When you take into account the bleakness of winter, it's no surprise that throughout history people have celebrated the winter solstice (the shortest day of the year), which heralds the arrival of longer days and the renewal of spring. Countless traditions are associated with midwinter celebrations. Here you'll find a brief explanation of why we celebrate in some of the ways that we do.

GIFTS

The tradition of gifts seems to have started with those that the wise men, or magi, brought to Jesus. Gift-giving at Christmas was rare in Europe or America before the 19th century, but the Santa Claus story, combined with an amazing retailing phenomenon that has grown over the past 100 years or so, has made giving gifts the central focus of the Christmas tradition. In the 19th century, gifts tended to be made by the giver and were practical, such as gloves or food, but modern gifts tend to be more frivolous, fun, or luxurious.

CHRISTMAS CARDS

Christmas cards were introduced in 1843 by Sir Henry Cole, an English businessman and patron of the arts, who printed 1,000 cards and sold them as a means of simplifying the sending of Christmas greetings. Nowadays, because we are all so busy, it's much more common for us to keep in touch with family and friends simply by mailing a card or even e-mailing greetings rather than buying a gift and giving it to them in person.

THE CHRISTMAS TREE

Ancient Egyptians used palms in their winter solstice festivals, and the Romans used firs, in anticipation of the lush greenery of spring with the return of the sun. Bringing an evergreen tree into the house was a long-standing German Christmas tradition, and the practice spread across America thanks to German immigrants. The Germans also decorated their trees with tinsel, fruits, pastries, candies, colored paper figures, tin angels, and other ornaments. Today, some form of Christmas tree, replete with all kinds of decorations, forms part of every Christmas celebration. And if you mount a star on top, it represents the star that led the wise men to the stable in Bethlehem.

Candles were traditionally placed in windows to help travelers to find houses in the dark, and to create festive cheer. Decorating houses, trees, and gardens with strings of multicolored lights for the Christmas period became popular in the 20th century.

CHRISTMAS WREATHS

In ancient Rome, people used decorative wreaths as a sign of victory and celebration, and the custom of hanging a Christmas wreath on the front door of the home probably started then. Today, there are two types of Christmas wreath: one that is made for decoration, and the other an advent wreath that has four colored candles lit on consecutive Sundays as a religious countdown to Christmas. The Christmas wreath symbolizes the strength of life overcoming the forces of winter. It is formed in a circle to signify eternity and usually hung on the front door to encourage happiness and good fortune in the New Year.

MISTLETOE AND HOLLY

These plants have long been associated with Christmas, and used in all types of decoration. Mistletoe is a symbol of peace and joy, and in ancient Britain, the Druids regarded it as sacred. Native Americans also regarded mistletoe as sacred, while the Scandinavians associated it with the goddess of love. The unholy and pagan associations with mistletoe (not forgetting the kissing, which is regarded as a sign of friendship and goodwill) caused the Church to ban its use and substitute holly instead, whose needlelike leaf points represented the crown of thorns Jesus wore when crucified; the red berries symbolized the drops of blood that He shed.

COLORS OF CHRISTMAS

The traditional colors of Christmas are green and red. Green represents the continuance of life through the winter and the Christian belief in eternal life through Christ. Red symbolizes the blood that Christians believe Jesus shed at his crucifixion.

ST NICHOLAS AND SANTA CLAUS

The transformation of St Nicholas to Santa Claus (or Father Christmas) happened largely in America. St Nicholas was a 4th-century Turkish bishop, whose reputation for generosity and kindness gave rise to all kinds of legends about miracles he performed. After the Reformation, Nicholas's cult disappeared in all the Protestant countries of Europe except Holland, where his legend persisted as Sinterklaas (a Dutch variant of the name St Nicholas). Dutch colonists took this tradition with them to the American colonies in the 17th century.

But the popular view of Santa that we all have today, along with the customary sleigh, the reindeer and the chimney, dates from the 19th century, when the poem "The Night Before Christmas" named the reindeer, invented the sleigh, and sent St Nicholas down the chimney. Also, a series of engravings run by a popular magazine of the time depicted a jolly Santa in his workshop, reading letters, checking his list, and so on. But the red and white suit did come from the original St Nicholas—those being the colors of a bishop's robes.

CHRISTMAS STOCKINGS

If you hang a stocking at the end of your bed or on your mantel, it's because of St Nicholas. According to legend, he took pity on a poverty-stricken family with three daughters who had no wedding dowries. For two of the daughters, he crept up to their house at night and threw bags of gold through a bedroom window. For the last daughter, he threw a bag of gold down the chimney, which landed in a stocking she had set by the fireplace for drying.

RUDOLF THE RED-NOSED REINDEER

The story of Rudolph, whose glowing nose is used as a navigational device, was created in 1939 by Robert May for a Chicago department store as a promotional gimmick. Johnny Marks, May's brother-in-law, eventually developed May's original story into lyrics and melody for a song, and Gene Autry's 1949 recording of it sold over 2 million copies, making it one of the best-selling Christmas records of all time.

CHRISTMAS MUSIC

Originally, carols were songs for celebration, and today they can include both religious songs, such as "Silent Night," as well as nonreligious songs like "Jingle Bells." Christmas music now includes classical pieces and pop and rock music. Bells are rung to announce the birth of Jesus, but may date back to pagan methods of warding off evil spirits.

ADVENT CALENDARS

Advent remains a season of spiritual preparation, and in many countries people use special calendars to count down to Christmas. A traditional advent calendar consists of two pieces of cardboard placed on top of each other. Twenty-four doors are cut out in the top layer, with one door being opened every day from December 1 until Christmas Eve to reveal a picture or a candy behind each compartment.

A Partridge in a Pear Tree

The English carol "The Twelve Days of Christmas" was supposedly created to keep the Catholic faith alive during a time of religious persecution—for example, the partridge was Jesus and the ten lords were the Ten Commandments. But it's more likely that it was just sung as an aid to help young children learn to count.

CREATING YOUR OWN TRADITIONS

If kissing under the mistletoe or singing carols around the Christmas tree just isn't your idea of fun, why not create some new customs for you to enjoy? You can make this season extra special if you take the time to create your own unique customs for you and your household.

The best way to do this is to hold a household meeting and get everyone to make a suggestion, then you can debate the merits of each. Possible options include:

★ A special book to read.

★ A family outing.

★ A classic movie to watch.

★ Making some edible treats together.

★ A countryside walk through the woods in search of reindeer on Christmas Eve.

★ Taking a photo of your children every year: date and frame them, then hang them on the tree, so that as they grow up, the children can see how much they've changed.

Countdown to
Christmas

This section deals with the practical aspects of Christmas, from how to organize your time, to shopping wisely, and choosing a tree. You'll also find a Christmas planning diary as well as useful advice for organizing a party.

ORGANIZING YOUR TIME

You don't need to start thinking about Christmas in July, but if you can start planning a few weeks ahead, it does make things easier. Find a calendar, notebook, and pen to plan out the vacation, then make a note of all the important dates such as school plays, concerts, church services, theater trips, and visits to relatives.

Get a folder for storing magazine articles, recipes, and any relevant notes—you can add to this each year with all sorts of ideas for gifts, crafts, parties, activities, and menus.

HOW TO AVOID CREDIT CARD DEBT

It's all too easy to get caught up in a frenzy of Christmas shopping and spend up to the limit on your credit cards, but with a little forethought you needn't end up in debt.

- Spread your Christmas spending throughout the year if you love to lavish family members with expensive gifts during the vacation and you don't want to stop the practice.
- Set aside a fixed amount each month to cover Christmas expenditure.
- Set a Christmas budget. Decide what you can reasonably afford to spend and do not go above that amount, even if it means sacrificing gifts along the way.
- Buy only for those closest to you.
- Shop around to find bargains and discounts throughout the year, and possibly wait for last-minute reductions.
- Save money and have fun at the same time by handcrafting some gifts or baking some edible gifts using the ideas in this book.

HOW TO CHOOSE A CHRISTMAS TREE

A favorite Christmas tradition is choosing and decorating your Christmas tree, and the main options are precut (convenient but costly) or cut-your-own (effort required). The major drawback to both precut and cut-your-own trees is that they are dead, so they will dry out and drop needles all over your floor and your gifts. And the drier they get, the more of a fire hazard they are. A potted tree is the freshest option, but then there's the problem of where to put it afterward. Or you could opt for an artificial tree—there are no worries over disposal, it will not shed needles and so create a mess, it's easy to store away, and you can use it again year after year.

* Know how tall your ceiling is and how much floor space you have available.
* If it will be on view from all sides, you'll want a symmetrical tree. If the tree will be going up against a wall, it doesn't matter if one side is less than perfect.
* Remember to take a tape measure with you to measure the tree.
* Look for a tree with a straight base, about 6-8 inches/15-20 cm long, so that you can make a fresh cut and still have room to fit it into your stand.
* Bear in mind the sturdiness of the branches. Many pines make tempting choices because of their long needles, but the branches will bend under the weight of even small ornaments.
* A fresh tree will look healthy and green, with few browning needles. The needles will feel pliable, and when broken and squeezed, they will exude pitch. To test whether a tree is fresh, carefully rub your hand along a branch to see if any needles fall off.

LOOKING AFTER YOUR TREE

The most important thing you can do is keep the tree watered. Make a fresh cut at the bottom of the tree at least 1 inch/2.5 cm above the original cut, then fill the reservoir with lukewarm water. Check and fill the reservoir often—Christmas trees become a fire hazard when their moisture content falls below 50 percent.

SAFETY TIPS

* Keep the tree away from open flames and other sources of heat. Even some appliances, like your TV, can heat up sufficiently to be hazardous.
* Keep tinsel away from light sockets.
* Always check your lights before you put them on the tree. Replace tree lights that have loose connections or exposed, brittle, or cracked wires, and never leave the lights on unattended.
* Don't leave light wires trailing along the floor for people to trip over.

Christmas Planner
Diary

During the vacation, there is plenty to organize and prepare, so it's a good idea to plan well in advance and then you will be ready for the big day when it arrives.

Checklist

WEEK 1 (END NOVEMBER/BEGINNING DECEMBER)
- Set your budget.
- Write your card list.
- Write your gift list and start buying gifts.
- Pack up and send overseas cards and gifts.
- Plan parties and activities for the season.

WEEK 2
- Presents—buy the biggest ones first so that you don't overspend on buying small gifts for others.
- Make your own Christmas cards and decorations if time allows.
- Get the Christmas decorations out of the attic, and test and replace Christmas lights if necessary.

WEEK 3
- Send off Christmas cards before the final post day.
- Finalize your Christmas menu.
- Buy plenty of wrapping paper and tape, and start wrapping gifts.

- Start a detailed grocery shopping list—put it up on the refrigerator and add to it as you think of items.
- Get the tree and decorate it—you could even hold a decorating party.

CHRISTMAS WEEK
- Tidy up your house and make sure the areas that are going to be in frequent use by guests (such as bathrooms) are sparkling clean.
- Hang up Christmas decorations.
- Put the gifts under the tree.
- Do the big Christmas food shop.

CHRISTMAS EVE
- Peel and cut all vegetables, and store in sealed containers in the refrigerator. Prepare and chill desserts, defrost the turkey, make seasoning mixes, and make or start accompanying sauces.
- Hang up the Christmas stockings and look forward to the big day tomorrow.

PARTY PLANNING

Whether it's a small gathering or a cast of hundreds, hosting a party is a great way to celebrate the vacation with friends and family. You don't need a degree in party planning to host a Christmas party, but you need more than a bottle of cooking sherry to make your guests rave about your merrymaking for months to come. Organization and careful planning are key to a great get-together. Organize everything in advance and create a detailed checklist, timetable, and to-do list. Constantly update your lists and keep all the papers together for quick reference. They can also form the basis for future party plans.

Set the budget. You need to know from the start how much you want to spend so that you don't have to cut back later. If you can afford only so much food or drink, then invite fewer guests rather than scrimping and saving—or, if you know your guests very well, ask them to contribute.

Food needs to look gorgeous, be appetizing, and taste delicious. Make sure you have plenty of options for vegetarians and guests on special or religious diets. Party food needs to be eaten easily with one hand, because your guests are bound to have a glass in the other, so keep the food very simple and preferably bite-size.

Don't rule out convenience foods and don't feel that everything has to be homemade—supplement a party buffet with a few store-bought crudités and dips, with plenty of fresh crusty bread, and a selection of cheeses in reserve. The idea is to minimize your efforts so that you haven't exhausted yourself before the party even begins.

Serve glasses of hot mulled wine for a festive feel and don't forget to offer plenty of nonalcoholic options, such as fresh fruit juices, sodas, cordials, and sparkling water. Try to keep your drinks selection simple, and allow for at least two glasses per person.

Finally, get yourself ready in plenty of time and be a guest at your own party rather than hiding in the kitchen. Smile and look as though you are enjoying yourself, and then everyone else will, too.

If you've got friends or family staying with you over the vacation, you'll probably feel the need to lay on a little festive entertainment. This doesn't have to be very elaborate or even obligatory, and need involve no more than a few board games, console or video games, or clearing a space for dancing. Try to set aside a suitable space in your home, such as the living room or conservatory, with perhaps a few bowls of nibbles to hand and a selection of sodas in the vicinity. If the weather is good, then outside activities could be as simple as a treasure hunt around the yard or in the local neighborhood.

Christmas Rec

CHAPTER 2

The excitement of preparations, the activity, the music, the lights, and the tantalizing aromas that pervade the home at this time of year all add to the magic of Christmas. Whether you are planning a small family get-together, a party for friends, or a much larger celebration, the following pages will help you plan and create the perfect Christmas feast.

The Christmas
Feast

The feast is the focal point of the celebrations. Although to some extent food is a significant part of all vacations, only Thanksgiving rivals the Christmas feast.

Christmas is traditionally a time of indulgence and good food, a time to ditch the diet and spoil yourself a little. December feasts have always been common in the northern hemisphere because in the old days it was necessary to slaughter cattle that would otherwise have been too expensive to feed during the winter,

and because the meat could be preserved by the cold weather. With the completion of the harvest and with snow on the ground, farmers were loaded with provisions. There was not much work that could be done, so it was an opportunity to relax, to feast, to celebrate, and to engage in social activities before the hard, lean months of winter set in.

The food that's traditionally on offer during the Christmas period reflects a particular country's climate and what's always been seasonally available, from dried fruits and nuts to root vegetables and fattened poultry, game, and meat. It's high-calorie food, too, because during the cold weather we need more calories just to stay warm, although that's not always the case in these days of central heating, so remember this when you reach for a third piece of apple pie!

There's a scrumptious array of mouthwatering food that's customarily eaten at Christmas, packed with robust flavors and enticing aromas. Food fashions come and go, but anyone planning a Christmas feast today would normally choose from appetizers such as shrimp cocktail, chicken liver pâté, or smoked salmon with cream cheese.

The centerpiece of the Christmas feast is usually a succulent turkey and a host of enticing seasonal vegetables on the side. Trimmings include Brussels sprouts with buttered chestnuts, glazed parsnips, cranberry sauce, and chestnut and sausage stuffing. Although turkey is the usual choice nowadays for Christmas lunch, there are numerous other traditional meat treats that you can enjoy, including game, goose, and duck, which are all at their best during Christmas. Glazed ham and poached salmon are also festive favorites, as is nut roast for vegetarians.

Desserts that are traditionally eaten during the festive period tend to be dense and calorie-laden, and include brandy snaps, baked Alaska, and pumpkin pie. And your waistband might expand even more with chocolate florentines, Christmas cake, chocolate Yule log, truffles, and lashings of brandy butter, to say nothing of a host of hearty alcoholic beverages, such as mulled wine or mulled ale, designed to warm you up and get you into the spirit of the season.

TOP TIPS WHEN PLANNING A CHRISTMAS FEAST

Planning a Christmas dinner isn't complicated, but the more forethought you give it, the easier it will be. The key is to do as much ahead of time as you can, to allow you to enjoy the big day.

- ✴ Decide how many guests you'll have, and work out how much space is available, both at the table and in your home.
- ✴ Draw up your menu and choose dishes that are both delicious and easy to make. Choose recipes that can be made ahead of time or that require just a little heating right before the feast to be completed. Another thing to remember when planning your menu is never choose a recipe that you have not tried before. Select reliable favorites, or, if you would like to add a new dish to your traditional menu, practice making it beforehand.
- ✴ Organize the menu into to-do lists, including all preparation steps.
- ✴ Empty as much of the refrigerator as possible.
- ✴ Make the big trip to the grocery store a few days in advance. Most items, with the exception of fruit and vegetables, will keep for a week.
- ✴ Set the table and get your home ready two days ahead, if seating people at a table for dinner. This will give you enough time to buy or borrow things you may need.
- ✴ Buffet service is easier to manage than seating everyone at the same table. Set the table against a wall and use it as the serving area. For a buffet, divide all the food into small portions.
- ✴ Plan your guests' arrival to give you enough time to cook.
- ✴ Serve some food that doesn't need to be cooked, like salad, cheese, and fresh fruit.

CAN YOUR KITCHEN COPE?

It's pointless to plan a feast that your kitchen can't handle. Every kitchen has space limitations; make sure you know yours. For example, is your cooker big enough to heat the five dishes you plan to serve hot at the same time? And how large is your refrigerator? Large enough to fit in all those platters of cold canapés? If not, now's the time to make adjustments and substitutions.

AVOID KITCHEN CHAOS Choose an array of foods served at a variety of temperatures and prepare as many dishes in advance as possible. Don't forget to allow enough time for defrosting and reheating your food on the day of the party.

Remember that food takes longer to cook when there are several dishes in the oven at the same time, so it's better to cook some food ahead and keep it warm rather than finding something is undercooked when you're ready to serve.

Line roasting trays with foil and discard at the end of cooking to make clearing up easier, and clear up as you go along to avoid accumulating a mountain of pots, pans, and kitchen clutter.

MAKE AS MUCH AHEAD AS YOU CAN Waiting until the last few days before your feast to cook everything just doesn't make sense, especially when, if you examine your menu, you'll see that much of it can be prepared ahead, frozen, and reheated. Just pin up a reminder to yourself so you don't forget to defrost in time.

Christmas cake can be made months ahead and is all the better for it, so set aside an afternoon for baking and roll up your sleeves. Cookie dough can be frozen for several weeks before you need it. If you're serving a decorated cake, make and bake the cake parts a week or more ahead of time, then wrap them well in plastic wrap and freeze them until the day before. Frozen cakes are easier to decorate than thawed ones anyway.

STORING FOOD If you run out of space, be creative. You can store food temporarily in the microwave or on top of the washing machine. If it's really cold outside, a garage can always serve as a second refrigerator.

TALKING TURKEY

If you know the size of bird you'll need and how to cook it, you're halfway to creating a successful Christmas dinner.

The amount of people you can feed with a particular bird will depend on how meaty it is, but as a rule of thumb a small turkey or goose will serve 4–7 people, a medium one 8–11, a large bird 12–15, and an extra-large turkey (over 17 lb 10 oz/ 8 kg) will serve up to 20.

For frozen birds, defrost in the refrigerator, allowing 18 hours per 2 lb 4 oz/1 kg, or in a cool place for 7 hours per 2 lb 4 oz/1 kg.

Cook the turkey up to an hour in advance and keep it warm by wrapping it in a double layer of foil, then cover it with a dish towel while other dishes are cooking to avoid last-minute panic.

Let the meat rest for at least 30 minutes before carving—this lets the juices settle back into the meat, making it more succulent and easier to carve.

DECORATING YOUR TABLE

A beautifully set table can make even plain food look elegant and inviting, and you don't need to spend a lot of money to do it. Start with a

tablecloth, especially if your dining-room table has seen better days. Tablecloths cover a multitude of sins while adding color and pattern. If you don't own the perfect tablecloth, rummage through thrift stores for old linens or even a beautiful sheet. Use prints sparingly though, to avoid the table looking too busy. Squares of silk can make a dramatic statement when artfully draped over a plain white tablecloth.

When it comes to centerpieces, don't limit your thinking to flowers, wreaths, or pine cones sprayed with gold and silver paint (although these are all attractive and festive decorations). A bowl of colorful fruits or vegetables such as kumquats or chile peppers, Christmas baubles, or even small bright toys can add charm and character to your table setting, depending on how you arrange them. If you are using foliage or fresh flowers, make sure they are clean before placing them near any food.

As for the rest of the table, it's up to you which china, glasswear, and flatware you use (matching if possible), whether to have festive napkin rings and place mats, or a selection of small personal gifts for your guests.

You just can't go wrong with candles. Candlelight is warm, cosy, and very festive. Avoid using scented candles because their fragrance may compete with the aromas of your Christmas cooking. Otherwise, candles of various heights look especially lovely when grouped together on mirrored surfaces (you could use a small wall mirror with the hanger on the back removed, or even a mirrored tile), and can form a backdrop to any number of different centerpieces. You can use either simple white candles in plain holders or candles in the traditional festive colors of red and green to add further color to your table.

Appetizers, Brunches, & Lunches

Wild Mushroom &

Sherry Soup

SERVES 4

2 tbsp olive oil
1 onion, chopped
1 garlic clove, chopped
4½ oz/125 g sweet potato,
   peeled and chopped
1 leek, trimmed and sliced
7 oz/200 g button and
   cremini mushrooms
5½ oz/150 g mixed
   wild mushrooms
2½ cups vegetable stock
1½ cups light cream
4 tbsp dry sherry
salt and pepper

FOR GARNISH
Parmesan cheese shavings
sautéed wild mushrooms, sliced

★ Heat the oil in a saucepan over medium heat. Add the onion and garlic and cook, stirring, for 3 minutes, until slightly softened. Add the sweet potato and cook, stirring, for 3 minutes. Add the leek and cook, stirring, for 2 minutes.

★ Stir in the mushrooms, stock, and cream. Bring to a boil, then reduce the heat and simmer gently, stirring occasionally, for 25 minutes. Remove from the heat, then stir in the sherry and let cool slightly.

★ Transfer half the soup to a food processor and blend until smooth. Return the mixture to the saucepan with the rest of the soup, then season with salt and pepper to taste, and reheat gently, stirring. Pour into 4 warmed soup bowls and garnish with Parmesan cheese shavings and sautéed wild mushrooms.

COOK'S NOTE

★ An increasing range of wild mushrooms is now available in grocery stores. If fresh ones are not available, use 1½–2 oz/40–55 g dried instead. Soak them in hot water for 30 minutes and drain well before using.

Spiced Pumpkin

Soup

SERVES 4

2 tbsp olive oil
1 onion, chopped
1 garlic clove, chopped
1 tbsp chopped fresh ginger
1 small red chile, seeded and finely
   chopped
2 tbsp chopped fresh cilantro
1 bay leaf
2 lb 4 oz/1 kg pumpkin, peeled,
   seeded, and diced
2½ cups vegetable stock
salt and pepper
light cream, for garnishing

★ Heat the oil in a saucepan over medium heat. Add the onion and garlic and cook, stirring, for 4 minutes, until slightly softened. Add the ginger, chile, cilantro, bay leaf, and pumpkin and cook, stirring, for 3 minutes.

★ Pour in the stock and bring to a boil. Using a slotted spoon, skim any scum from the surface. Reduce the heat and simmer gently, stirring occasionally, for 25 minutes, or until the pumpkin is tender. Remove from the heat, then take out and discard the bay leaf. Let cool slightly.

★ Transfer the soup to a food processor and blend until smooth (you may have to do this in batches). Return the mixture to the saucepan and season with salt and pepper to taste. Reheat gently, stirring. Remove from the heat, and pour into 4 warmed soup bowls. Garnish each one with a swirl of cream, then serve.

COOK'S NOTE

★ Even so-called pie pumpkins are often larger than required, so you may need to buy a section of a larger one to avoid waste (they are often sold by the piece). Check that the flesh is firm and has not dried out and become unpleasantly fibrous.

Mozzarella Crostini
with Pesto & Caviar

SERVES 4

8 slices white bread,
  crusts removed
3 tbsp olive oil
7 oz/200 g firm mozzarella
  cheese, diced
6 tbsp lumpfish roe

PESTO
2 ³/₄ oz/75 g fresh basil,
  finely chopped
¹/₃ cup pine nuts,
  finely chopped
2 garlic cloves, finely chopped
3 tbsp olive oil

★ Preheat the oven to 350°F/180°C. Using a sharp knife, cut the bread into fancy shapes, such as half-moons, stars, and Christmas trees. Drizzle with the oil, then transfer to an ovenproof dish and bake in the preheated oven for 15 minutes.

★ While the bread is baking, make the pesto. Put the basil, pine nuts, and garlic in a small bowl. Pour in the oil and stir well.

★ Remove the bread shapes from the oven and let cool. Spread a layer of pesto on the shapes and top each one with a piece of mozzarella and some lumpfish roe, then serve.

COOK'S NOTE

★ Lumpfish roe is often colored black to resemble caviar, although it may also be dyed orange or red. The color tends to run, so do not top the crostini until you are ready to serve. You could use naturally colored roes, such as keta salmon roe or trout roe, which do not run.

Chicken Liver

Pâté

SERVES 4–6

scant 1 cup butter
8 oz/225 g trimmed chicken
   livers, thawed if frozen
2 tbsp Marsala wine or brandy
1½ tsp chopped fresh sage
1 garlic clove, coarsely chopped
⅔ cup heavy cream
salt and pepper
fresh bay leaves or sage leaves,
   for garnishing
Melba toast (see Cook's Note,
   below), for serving

★ Melt 3 tablespoons of the butter in a large, heavy-bottom skillet. Add the chicken livers and cook over medium heat for 4 minutes on each side. They should be browned on the outside but still pink in the center. Transfer to a food processor and process until finely chopped.

★ Stir the Marsala into the skillet, scraping up any sediment with a wooden spoon, then add to the food processor with the chopped sage, garlic, and 7 tablespoons of the remaining butter. Process until smooth. Add the cream and season with salt and pepper to taste, then process until thoroughly combined and smooth. Spoon the pâté into a dish or individual ramekins and level the surface, then let cool completely.

★ Melt the remaining butter in a small saucepan, then spoon it over the surface of the pâté, leaving any sediment in the pan. Garnish with herb leaves and let cool, then cover and chill in the refrigerator. Serve with Melba toast.

COOK'S NOTE

★ To make Melba toast, broil slices of white bread on both sides until golden. Cut off and discard the crusts and slice the bread in half horizontally. Broil the cut sides until golden and the edges are curling. Cool and store in an airtight container until required.

Festive Shrimp *Cocktail*

SERVES 8

½ cup tomato ketchup
1 tsp chili sauce
1 tsp Worcestershire sauce
2 lb 4 oz/1 kg cooked jumbo
   shrimp
2 ruby grapefruits
lettuce leaves, shredded
2 avocados, peeled, pitted,
   and diced

MAYONNAISE
2 large egg yolks
1 tsp mustard powder
1 tsp salt
1¼ cups peanut oil
1 tsp white wine vinegar
pepper

FOR GARNISH
lime slices
fresh dill sprigs

 First make the mayonnaise. Put the egg yolks in a bowl and add the mustard powder, pepper to taste, and salt, then beat together well. Pour the oil into a pitcher and make sure that your bowl is secure on the counter by sitting it on a damp cloth. Using an electric or hand whisk, begin to whisk the egg yolks, adding just 1 drop of the oil. Make sure that this has been thoroughly absorbed before adding another drop and whisking well.

 Continue adding the oil 1 drop at a time until the mixture thickens and stiffens—at this point, whisk in the vinegar, and then continue to dribble in the remaining oil very slowly in a thin stream, whisking continuously, until you have used up all the oil and you have a thick mayonnaise.

 Mix the mayonnaise, tomato ketchup, chili sauce, and Worcestershire sauce together in a small bowl. Cover with plastic wrap and refrigerate until required.

 Remove the heads from the shrimp and peel off the shells, leaving the tails intact. Slit along the length of the back of each shrimp with a sharp knife and remove and discard the dark vein. Cut off a slice from the top and bottom of each grapefruit, then peel off the skin and all the white pith. Cut between the membranes to separate the segments.

 When ready to serve, make a bed of shredded lettuce in the base of 8 glass dishes. Divide the shrimp, grapefruit segments, and avocados among them and spoon over the mayonnaise dressing. Serve the cocktails garnished with lime slices and dill sprigs.

Turkey Club
Sandwiches

SERVES 6

SANDWICHES
12 pancetta or bacon slices
18 slices white bread
12 slices cooked turkey
    breast meat
3 plum tomatoes, sliced
6 Boston lettuce leaves
6 stuffed olives
salt and pepper

MAYONNAISE
2 large egg yolks
1 tsp mustard powder
1 tsp salt
1¼ cups peanut oil
1 tsp white wine vinegar
pepper

✦ First make the mayonnaise. Put the egg yolks in a bowl and add the mustard powder, pepper to taste, and salt, then beat together well. Pour the oil into a pitcher and make sure that your bowl is secure on the counter by sitting it on a damp cloth. Using an electric or hand whisk, begin to whisk the egg yolks, adding just 1 drop of the oil. Make sure that this has been thoroughly absorbed before adding another drop and whisking well.

✦ Continue adding the oil 1 drop at a time until the mixture thickens and stiffens—at this point, whisk in the vinegar and then continue to dribble in the remaining oil very slowly in a thin stream, whisking continuously, until you have used up all the oil and you have a thick mayonnaise. Cover and refrigerate while you prepare the other sandwich components.

✦ Broil or fry the pancetta until crisp, then drain on paper towels and keep warm. Toast the bread until golden, then cut off the crusts.

✦ You will need 3 slices of toast for each sandwich. For each sandwich, spread the first piece of toast with a generous amount of mayonnaise, then top with 2 slices of turkey, keeping the edges neat, and top with a couple of slices of tomato. Season with salt and pepper to taste. Add another slice of toast and top with 2 pancetta slices and 1 lettuce leaf. Season again with salt and pepper to taste and add a little more mayonnaise, then top with the final piece of toast. Push a toothpick or a decorative sparkler through a stuffed olive, and then push this through the sandwich to hold it together.

Blinis with Shrimp &
Wasabi Cream

SERVES 6

2½ cups all-purpose flour
scant 1 cup buckwheat flour
2 tsp active dry yeast
2½ cups whole milk, warmed
6 eggs, separated
3 tbsp unsalted butter, melted
5 tbsp sour cream
3½ tbsp clarified butter
salt

WASABI CREAM
scant 1 cup sour cream
½ tsp wasabi paste, or to taste

FOR SERVING
10½ oz/300 g cooked shrimp,
   peeled and deveined
1¾ oz/50 g pickled ginger,
   thinly sliced
2 tbsp fresh cilantro leaves

★ Sift the flours together into a large bowl and stir in the yeast. Make a hollow in the center and add the milk, then gradually beat in the flour until you have a smooth batter. Cover and chill in the refrigerator overnight.

★ Two hours before you need the blinis, remove the bowl from the refrigerator and set the batter aside for 1 hour 20 minutes to return to room temperature. Beat in the egg yolks, melted butter, and sour cream. In a separate bowl, whisk the egg whites until stiff, then gradually fold into the batter. Cover and let rest for 30 minutes.

★ Meanwhile, make the wasabi cream. Mix the sour cream and wasabi paste together in a small bowl until completely combined. Taste and add a little more wasabi paste if you like it hotter. Season with salt only to taste, then cover and chill in the refrigerator.

★ To cook the blinis, heat a little of the clarified butter in a nonstick skillet over medium-high heat. When hot and sizzling, drop in 3–4 tablespoonfuls of the batter, spaced well apart, and cook until puffed up and bubbles appear around the edges. Flip them over and cook for a few more minutes on the other side. Remove from the skillet and keep warm while you cook the remaining batter.

★ To serve, spoon a little of the wasabi cream onto a blini. Add 1 or 2 shrimp and a little ginger, then scatter with a few cilantro leaves.

Smoked Salmon
Risotto

SERVES 4

3½ tbsp unsalted butter
1 onion, finely chopped
½ small fennel bulb,
    very finely chopped
1 lb 2 oz/500 g Arborio or
    carnaroli rice
1¼ cups white wine
    or vermouth
5 cups hot fish stock
5½ oz/150 g hot smoked
    salmon flakes
5½ oz/150 g smoked
    salmon slices
2 tbsp fresh chervil leaves or
    chopped flat-leaf parsley
salt and pepper

★ Melt half the butter in a large saucepan over medium heat. Add the onion and fennel, and cook, stirring frequently, for 5 to 8 minutes, until transparent and soft. Add the rice and stir well to coat the grains in the butter. Cook, stirring, for 3 minutes, then add the wine, stir, and let simmer until most of the liquid has been absorbed.

★ With the stock simmering in a separate saucepan, add 1 ladleful to the rice and stir well. Cook, stirring continuously, until nearly all the liquid has been absorbed before adding another ladleful of stock. Continue to add the remaining stock in the same way until the rice is cooked al dente and most or all of the stock has been added.

★ Remove from the heat and stir in the two types of salmon and the remaining butter, then season with salt and pepper to taste. Serve scattered with the chervil or parsley.

COOK'S NOTE

★ This risotto can be made with cooked shrimp or other seafood—try it with crabmeat and saffron.

Roast Squash with
Cranberries

SERVES 4

4 acorn or small butternut squash
½ cup basmati rice
¼ cup wild rice
2 tbsp butter
1 tbsp olive oil, plus extra
    for oiling
1 red onion, thinly sliced
2 garlic cloves, crushed
1 cup dried cranberries
⅓ cup pine nuts, toasted
2 tbsp fresh parsley,
    finely chopped
whole nutmeg, for grating
scant 1½ cups fresh white or whole
    wheat breadcrumbs
1 oz/25 g Parmesan cheese,
    finely grated
butter, for dotting
salt and pepper

★ If using acorn squash, cut through the center and trim the stalk and root so that the squash will stand upright securely, then scoop out and discard the seeds. If using butternut squash, cut lengthwise in half and scoop out and discard the seeds. Place the prepared squash on an oiled baking sheet.

★ Cook the two types of rice separately according to the package directions and drain well.

★ Meanwhile, preheat the oven to 375°F/190°C. Melt the butter with the oil in a skillet over medium heat. Add the onion and garlic, then cook, stirring frequently, for 8 minutes, until transparent and soft.

★ Tip all the cooked rice and the cooked onion and garlic into a bowl. Add the cranberries, pine nuts, and parsley, then grate in a little nutmeg and season with salt and pepper to taste. Mix together well.

★ Carefully divide the stuffing mixture among the squash, then top with the breadcrumbs and Parmesan cheese and dot with butter. Bake in the preheated oven for 50 minutes, then serve hot.

COOK'S NOTE

★ You can vary the stuffing ingredients and use other nuts such as walnuts or almonds and replace the cranberries with chopped plumped dried apricots.

Chestnut, Madeira, & *Mushroom Tarts*

MAKES 12

PIE DOUGH
7 tbsp unsalted butter, chilled and diced, plus extra for greasing
scant 1¾ cups all-purpose flour, plus extra for dusting
pinch of salt

FILLING
2 tbsp unsalted butter
1 tsp olive oil
1 shallot, finely chopped
1 garlic clove, crushed
8 cooked chestnuts, peeled and coarsely chopped
7 oz/200 g cremini mushrooms, chopped
2 tbsp Madeira
⅔ cup heavy cream
1 egg, plus 1 egg yolk
salt and pepper
chopped fresh parsley, for serving

✴ Lightly grease a 3-inch/7.5-cm, 12-cup muffin pan with butter. Sift the flour into a large bowl and add the salt, then rub in the remaining butter until the mixture resembles breadcrumbs. Add a little cold water—just enough to bring the dough together. Knead the dough briefly on a floured counter.

✴ Divide the pie dough in half. Roll out 1 piece of dough and, using a 3½-inch/9-cm plain dough cutter, cut out 6 rounds, then roll each round into a 4½-inch/12-cm round. Repeat with the remaining dough until you have 12 rounds of dough, then use to line the muffin pan. Chill in the refrigerator for 30 minutes.

✴ Meanwhile, preheat the oven to 400°F/200°C and make the filling. Melt the butter with the oil in a small skillet over low heat. Add the shallot and garlic, then cook, stirring occasionally, for 5 to 8 minutes, until the shallot is transparent and soft. Add the chestnuts and mushrooms and cook, stirring, for 2 minutes, then add the Madeira and simmer for 2 minutes.

✴ Line the pastry shells with parchment paper and fill with dried beans, then bake in the preheated oven for 10 minutes. Carefully lift out the paper and beans, and reduce the oven temperature to 375°F/190°C. Stir the cream, whole egg, and egg yolk into the mushroom mixture and season well with salt and pepper. Divide among the pastry shells and bake for 10 minutes. Let cool in the pan for 5 minutes, then carefully remove from the pan. Scatter with chopped parsley and serve.

Double Cheese
Souffles

MAKES 6

2 tbsp butter, plus extra
    for greasing
2 tbsp finely grated Parmesan
    cheese
¾ cup milk
scant ¼ cup self-rising flour
whole nutmeg, for grating
3½ oz/100 g soft goat cheese
2½ oz/70 g sharp cheddar cheese,
    grated
2 large eggs, separated
salt and pepper

★ Preheat the oven to 400°F/200°C. Put a baking sheet in the oven to warm. Generously grease the inside of 6 small ramekins with butter, then add half the Parmesan cheese and shake to coat the butter.

★ Warm the milk in a small saucepan. Melt the remaining butter in a separate saucepan over medium heat. Add the flour and stir well to combine, then cook, stirring, for 2 minutes, until smooth. Add a little of the warmed milk and stir until absorbed. Continue to add the milk a little at a time, stirring continuously, until you have a rich, smooth sauce. Season with salt and pepper to taste, and grate in a little nutmeg. Add the cheeses to the sauce and stir until well combined and melted.

★ Remove from the heat and set the sauce aside to cool a little, then add the egg yolks and stir to combine. In a separate bowl, whisk the egg whites until stiff. Fold a tablespoonful of the egg whites into the cheese sauce, then gradually fold in the remaining egg whites. Spoon into the prepared ramekins and scatter over the remaining Parmesan cheese.

★ Place the ramekins on the hot baking sheet and bake in the preheated oven for 15 minutes, until puffed up and brown. Remove from the oven and serve immediately. The soufflés will collapse quite quickly when taken from the oven, so have your serving plates ready to take the soufflés to the table.

COOK'S NOTE
★ You can vary the cheeses, but always choose a full-flavored, hard cheese to complement the goat cheese.

Main Courses &

Accompaniments

Roast Turkey with

Bread Sauce

SERVES 8

1 quantity Chestnut and
   Sausage Stuffing
one 11-lb/5-kg turkey
3 tbsp butter

BREAD SAUCE
1 onion, peeled
4 cloves
2½ cups milk
2⅓ cups fresh white
   breadcrumbs
4 tbsp butter
salt and pepper

★ Preheat the oven to 425°F/220°C. Spoon the stuffing into the neck cavity of the turkey and close the flap of skin with a skewer. Place the bird in a large roasting pan and rub it all over with the butter. Roast in the preheated oven for 1 hour, then reduce the oven temperature to 350°F/180°C and roast for an additional 2½ hours. You may need to pour off the fat from the pan occasionally.

★ Meanwhile, make the bread sauce. Stud the onion with the cloves, then place in a saucepan with the milk, breadcrumbs, and butter. Bring just to boiling point over low heat, then remove from the heat and let stand in a warm place to infuse. Just before serving, remove the onion and cloves and reheat the sauce gently, beating well with a wooden spoon. Season with salt and pepper to taste.

★ Check that the turkey is cooked by inserting a skewer or the point of a sharp knife into the thigh—if the juices run clear, it is ready. Transfer the bird to a carving board and cover loosely with foil, then let rest.

★ Carve the turkey and serve with the warm bread sauce.

Yuletide Goose with
Honey & Pears

SERVES 4–6

one 7¾–10-lb/3.5–4.5-kg
  oven-ready goose
1 tsp salt
4 pears
1 tbsp lemon juice
4 tbsp butter
2 tbsp honey

★ Preheat the oven to 425°F/220°C. Rinse the goose and pat dry. Use a fork to prick the skin all over, then rub with the salt. Place the bird upside down on a rack in a roasting pan. Roast in the preheated oven for 30 minutes. Drain off the fat. Turn the bird over and roast for 15 minutes. Drain off the fat.

★ Reduce the oven temperature to 350°F/180°C and roast for 15 minutes per 1 lb/450 g. Cover with foil 15 minutes before the end of the cooking time. Check that the bird is cooked by inserting a knife between the legs and body. If the juices run clear, it is cooked. Remove from the oven. Transfer the goose to a warmed serving platter and cover loosely with foil, then let rest.

★ Peel and halve the pears, then brush with the lemon juice. Melt the butter and honey in a saucepan over low heat, then add the pears. Cook, stirring, for 5 to 10 minutes, until tender. Remove from the heat, then arrange the pears around the goose. Pour the sweet juices over the bird, then serve.

COOK'S NOTE

★ "Christmas is coming and the goose is getting fat"–and they do look like extremely big birds. However, there is proportionately a lot less meat on a goose than on a turkey or chicken because a goose's rib cage is so large.

Baked

Ham

SERVES 8

one 8¾-lb/4-kg ham joint
1 apple, cored and chopped
1 onion, chopped
1¼ cups hard cider
6 black peppercorns
1 bouquet garni
1 bay leaf
about 50 cloves
4 tbsp raw brown sugar

★ Put the ham in a large saucepan and add enough cold water to cover. Bring to a boil and skim off the scum that rises to the surface. Reduce the heat and simmer for 30 minutes. Drain the ham and return to the saucepan. Add the apple, onion, cider, peppercorns, bouquet garni, bay leaf, and a few of the cloves. Pour in enough fresh water to cover and return to a boil. Reduce the heat, then cover and simmer for 3 hours 20 minutes.

★ Preheat the oven to 400°F/200°C. Take the saucepan off the heat and set aside to cool slightly. Remove the ham from the cooking liquid and, while it is still warm, loosen the rind with a sharp knife, then peel it off and discard. Score the fat into diamond shapes and stud with the remaining cloves. Place the ham on a rack in a roasting pan and sprinkle with the sugar. Roast in the oven, basting occasionally with the cooking liquid, for 20 minutes. Serve hot, or cold later.

COOK'S NOTE

★ You can buy prepared bouquet garni in little envelopes like teabags. However, fresh herbs are much more flavorsome. Tie together 2-3 fresh parsley sprigs, 1 fresh thyme sprig, and a fresh bay leaf into a bundle. For extra flavor, tie them together with a strip of celery rather than string.

Roast Pheasant with
Wine & Herbs

SERVES 4

7 tbsp butter,
    slightly softened
1 tbsp chopped fresh thyme
1 tbsp chopped fresh parsley
2 oven-ready young pheasants
4 tbsp vegetable oil
½ cup red wine
salt and pepper
game fries (see Cook's Note,
    below), for serving

★ Preheat the oven to 375°F/190°C. Put the butter in a small bowl and mix in the chopped herbs. Lift the skins off the pheasants, taking care not to tear them, and push the herb butter under the skins. Season with salt and pepper to taste. Pour the oil into a roasting pan, then add the pheasants and roast in the preheated oven for 45 minutes, basting occasionally. Remove from the oven and pour over the wine, then return to the oven and cook for an additional 15 minutes, until cooked through. Check that each bird is cooked by inserting a knife between the legs and body. If the juices run clear, they are cooked.

★ Remove the pheasants from the oven and cover loosely with foil, then let rest for 15 minutes. Serve on a warmed serving platter surrounded with game fries.

COOK'S NOTE

★ To make game fries, peel 1½ lb/650 g potatoes and cut into wafer-thin slices. Immediately place in a bowl of cold water. Heat sunflower or corn oil in a deep-fryer to 375°F/190°C, or until a cube of day-old bread browns in 30 seconds. Drain the potato slices and pat dry with paper towels. Deep-fry, in batches, for 2 to 3 minutes, stirring to prevent them from sticking, and remove with a slotted spoon. Drain on paper towels and keep warm while you cook the remaining slices.

Festive Beef

Wellington

SERVES 4

1 lb 10 oz/750 g thick beef
    tenderloin
2 tbsp butter
2 tbsp vegetable oil
1 garlic clove, chopped
1 onion, chopped
6 oz/175 g cremini mushrooms,
    thinly sliced
1 tbsp chopped fresh sage
12 oz/350 g puff pastry,
    thawed if frozen
1 egg, beaten
salt and pepper

 Preheat the oven to 425°F/220°C. Put the beef in a roasting pan and spread with the butter, then season with salt and pepper to taste. Roast in the preheated oven for 30 minutes, then remove from the oven.

 Meanwhile, heat the oil in a saucepan over medium heat. Add the garlic and onion and cook, stirring, for 3 minutes. Stir in salt and pepper to taste, the mushrooms, and the sage and cook, stirring frequently, for 5 minutes. Remove from the heat.

 Roll out the pastry into a rectangle large enough to enclose the beef, then place the beef in the center and spread the mushroom mixture over it. Bring the long sides of the pastry together over the beef and seal with beaten egg. Tuck the short ends over (trim away excess pastry) and seal. Place on a baking sheet, seam-side down. Make 2 slits in the top. Decorate with pastry shapes and brush with egg. Bake for 40 minutes. Remove from the oven and cut into thick slices, then serve.

COOK'S NOTE

 Frozen puff pastry should be thawed before use, but make sure that it is well chilled in the refrigerator before rolling out. This helps to ensure that the layers puff up during cooking. If the pastry browns too quickly in the oven, cover with foil.

Poached
Salmon

SERVES 8–12

4¼ quarts water
6 tbsp white wine vinegar
1 large onion, sliced
2 carrots, sliced
1½ tbsp salt
1 tsp black peppercorns
one 6-lb/2.7-kg salmon, cleaned,
   with gills and eyes removed

FOR SERVING
green salad
1 cucumber, thinly sliced
lemon wedges

★ To make a court-bouillon (stock) in which to poach the fish, put the water, vinegar, onion, carrots, salt, and peppercorns in a large fish kettle or covered roasting pan and bring to a boil. Reduce the heat and simmer for 20 minutes. Remove the trivet (if using a fish kettle) and lay the salmon on it. Lower it into the court-bouillon and cover, then return to simmering point and cook for 5 minutes. Turn off the heat and set aside the fish, covered, to cool in the liquid.

★ When the fish is cold, lift it out of the kettle on the trivet and drain well. Using 2 spatulas, carefully transfer to a board. Using a sharp knife, remove the head, then slit the skin along the backbone and peel off. Carefully turn the fish over and peel off the skin on the other side.

★ To serve, line a serving platter with green salad and cucumber and carefully transfer the salmon to the platter. Serve with lemon wedges.

COOK'S NOTE

★ This easy dish is a great choice for a Christmas Eve dinner party or for a cold buffet on Christmas day. It is prepared in advance and provides a welcome contrast to the prodigious quantities of meat often consumed at this time of year. It also looks and tastes rather special.

Duck with Madeira &

Blueberry Sauce

SERVES 4

4 duck breasts (skin left on)
4 garlic cloves, chopped
grated rind and juice of 1 orange
1 tbsp chopped fresh parsley
salt and pepper

**MADEIRA AND
BLUEBERRY SAUCE**
1 cup blueberries
1 cup Madeira
1 tbsp red currant preserve

FOR SERVING
new potatoes
selection of green vegetables

✷ Use a sharp knife to make several shallow diagonal cuts in each duck breast. Put the duck in a glass bowl with the garlic, orange rind and juice, and the parsley. Season with salt and pepper to taste and stir well. Turn the duck in the mixture until thoroughly coated. Cover the bowl with plastic wrap and set aside in the refrigerator to marinate for at least 1 hour.

✷ Heat a dry, nonstick skillet over medium heat. Add the duck breasts and cook for 4 minutes, then turn them over and cook for an additional 4 minutes, or according to taste. Remove from the heat and cover the skillet, then let stand for 5 minutes.

✷ Halfway through the cooking time, put the blueberries, Madeira, and red currant preserve into a separate saucepan. Bring to a boil. Reduce the heat and simmer for 10 minutes, then remove from the heat.

✷ Slice the duck breasts and transfer to warmed serving plates. Serve with the sauce poured over and accompanied by new potatoes and a selection of green vegetables.

COOK'S NOTE

✷ Duck has a reputation for being a very fatty meat, but modern breeders are producing much leaner birds these days. The meat, therefore, needs careful cooking to prevent it from drying out and losing its texture.

Chicken
Roulades

SERVES 6

6 skinless, boneless chicken
    breasts, about 6 oz/175 g each
scant 1 cup fresh ground chicken
1 tbsp olive oil
2 shallots, coarsely chopped
1 garlic clove, crushed
2/3 cup heavy cream
3 fresh sage leaves, chopped
1 tbsp chopped fresh parsley
1 tbsp cognac or sherry
1 tbsp vegetable oil
18 pancetta slices
1 dessertspoon all-purpose flour
scant 1 cup white wine
scant 1 cup chicken stock
salt and pepper
Parsnip and Potato Cakes, to serve

✷ Place a chicken breast between 2 pieces of plastic wrap and, using a rolling pin, flatten the breast as evenly as possible. Trim off the rough edges to make a neat square. Repeat with the remaining breasts, then cover and chill.

✷ Meanwhile, chop the chicken trimmings and mix with the ground chicken in a bowl. Heat the olive oil in a small skillet over medium heat, then add the shallots and garlic, and cook, stirring frequently, for 5 minutes. Add to the ground chicken with the cream, herbs, and cognac and mix together thoroughly. Season with salt and pepper to taste. Cover and chill in the refrigerator for 15 minutes.

✷ Bring a large saucepan of water to a boil, then reduce to a simmer. Divide the ground chicken mixture among the breasts and spread to within ½ inch/1 cm of the edge, then roll each breast up to form a sausage shape. Wrap each roll tightly in aluminum foil, securing both ends. Poach in the simmering water for 20 minutes, then remove with a slotted spoon and let cool completely.

✷ Meanwhile, preheat the oven to 375°F/190°C. Put the vegetable oil in a roasting pan and heat in the oven. Remove the aluminum foil and wrap each roulade tightly in 3 pancetta slices. Carefully roll in the hot oil, then roast in the oven for 25 to 30 minutes, turning twice, until they are browned and crisp. Remove the roulades from the pan and keep warm. Place the pan on the stove, then add the flour and stir well with a wooden spoon to form a smooth paste. Gradually whisk in the wine and stock. Let bubble for 4 to 5 minutes, then season with salt and pepper to taste. Slice the roulades and serve with Parsnip and Potato Cakes and gravy.

Traditional
Roast Chicken

SERVES 6

one 5-lb/2.25-kg free-range
   chicken
4 tbsp butter
2 tbsp chopped fresh lemon thyme
1 lemon, quartered
½ cup white wine
salt and pepper
6 fresh thyme sprigs, for
   garnishing

★ Preheat the oven to 425°F/220°C. Make sure the chicken is clean, wiping it inside and out with paper towels, and place in a roasting pan. In a bowl, soften the butter with a fork, mix in the thyme, and season well with salt and pepper. Butter the chicken all over with the herb butter, inside and out, and place the lemon pieces inside the body cavity. Pour the wine over the chicken.

★ Roast in the center of the preheated oven for 20 minutes. Reduce the oven temperature to 375°F/190°C and roast for an additional 1¼ hours, basting frequently. Cover with foil if the skin begins to brown too much. If the pan dries out, add a little more wine or water.

★ Test that the chicken is cooked by piercing the thickest part of the leg with a sharp knife or skewer and making sure the juices run clear. Remove from the oven. Transfer the chicken to a warmed serving plate, then cover loosely with foil and let rest for 10 minutes before carving. Place the roasting pan on the top of the stove and bubble the pan juices gently over low heat until they have reduced and are thick and glossy. Season with salt and pepper to taste. Serve the chicken with the pan juices and scatter with the thyme sprigs.

COOK'S NOTE

★ Chicken has become a well-established favorite in recent years, although it was once seen as quite exclusive. Simply roasted, with plenty of thyme and lemon, chicken produces a succulent gastronomic feast for many occasions. You can stuff your chicken with a traditional stuffing, such as sage and onion, or with fruit like apricots and prunes, but often the best way is to keep it simple. If you do stuff the chicken, remember to stuff just the neck end, not the whole cavity, or the bird might not cook all the way through.

Herbed Salmon with

Hollandaise Sauce

SERVES 4

4 salmon fillets, about 6 oz/
   175 g each, skin removed
2 tbsp olive oil
1 tbsp chopped fresh dill
1 tbsp snipped fresh chives,
   plus extra for garnishing
salt and pepper

HOLLANDAISE SAUCE
3 egg yolks
1 tbsp water
1 cup butter, cut into
   small cubes
juice of 1 lemon
salt and pepper

FOR SERVING
freshly cooked sprouting broccoli
sesame seeds

★ Preheat the broiler to medium. Rinse the fish fillets under cold running water and pat dry with paper towels. Season with salt and pepper to taste. Combine the oil with the dill and chives in a bowl, then brush the mixture over the fish. Transfer to the broiler and cook for 6 to 8 minutes, turning once and brushing with more oil and herb mixture, until cooked to your taste.

★ Meanwhile, make the sauce. Put the egg yolks in a heatproof bowl over a saucepan of gently simmering water (or use a double boiler). Add the water and season with salt and pepper to taste. Reduce the heat until the water in the saucepan is barely simmering and whisk continuously until the mixture begins to thicken. Whisk in the butter, one piece at a time, until the mixture is thick and shiny. Whisk in the lemon juice, then remove from the heat.

★ Remove the salmon from the broiler and transfer to warmed individual serving plates. Pour the sauce over the fish and garnish with snipped fresh chives. Serve immediately on a bed of sprouting broccoli, garnished with sesame seeds.

COOK'S NOTE

★ Do not let the base of the bowl touch the surface of the water when you are making the sauce, or the egg yolks may curdle. It is also important that the water is barely simmering rather than boiling vigorously.

Mixed Nut Roast with

Cranberry Sauce

SERVES 4

2 tbsp butter, plus extra
   for greasing
2 garlic cloves, chopped
1 large onion, chopped
⅓ cup pine nuts, toasted
½ cup hazelnuts, toasted
½ cup walnuts, ground
½ cup cashew nuts, ground
2 cups fresh whole wheat
   breadcrumbs
1 egg, lightly beaten
2 tbsp chopped fresh thyme
heaping 1 cup vegetable stock
salt and pepper
fresh thyme sprigs, for garnishing

CRANBERRY SAUCE
scant 1 cup fresh cranberries
½ cup superfine sugar
1¼ cups red wine
1 cinnamon stick

★ Preheat the oven to 350°F/180°C. Grease a loaf pan with butter and line it with wax paper. Melt the remaining butter in a saucepan over medium heat. Add the garlic and onion and cook, stirring, for 5 minutes, until softened. Remove from the heat. Grind the pine nuts and hazelnuts. Stir all the nuts into the saucepan, then add the breadcrumbs, egg, thyme, and stock and season with salt and pepper to taste.

★ Spoon the mixture into the loaf pan and level the surface. Cook in the preheated oven for 30 minutes, until cooked through and golden. The loaf is cooked when a skewer inserted into the center comes out clean.

★ Halfway through the cooking time, make the sauce. Put all the ingredients in a saucepan and bring to a boil. Reduce the heat and simmer gently, stirring occasionally, for 15 minutes.

★ To serve, remove the sauce from the heat and discard the cinnamon stick. Remove the nut roast from the oven and turn out onto a warmed serving dish. Garnish with thyme sprigs and serve with the sauce.

COOK'S NOTE

★ Nuts contain a lot of oil and will turn rancid if they are stored too long. Buy them in small quantities and store in airtight containers, keeping an eye on the expiration dates. It is worth buying fresh nuts for this festive treat.

Beef with Pancakes &

Mustard Sauce

SERVES 6

6 beef tenderloins, about
    5½ oz/150 g each
1 tbsp olive oil
1 tsp unsalted butter
scant 1 cup sour cream
2 tsp whole grain mustard
2 tbsp snipped fresh chives
salt and pepper

PANCAKES
14 oz/400 g potatoes
⅓ cup self-rising flour
½ tsp baking powder
scant 1 cup milk
2 eggs, beaten
vegetable oil, for frying

★ To make the pancakes, cook the potatoes in their skins in a large saucepan of boiling water until tender. Drain and set aside until cool enough to handle. Peel, then mash and press through a strainer, into a bowl.

★ Sift the flour and baking powder over the potatoes, then add a little of the milk and mix well. Add the remaining milk and the eggs and beat well to make a smooth batter.

★ Heat a little vegetable oil in an 8-inch/20-cm nonstick skillet over medium heat. Add a ladleful of the batter to cover the bottom of the skillet and cook until little bubbles appear on the surface. Turn over and cook for an additional minute, or until nicely browned, then turn out and keep warm. Repeat until you have cooked 6 pancakes.

★ Season the beef tenderloins with salt and pepper to taste. Heat the olive oil and butter in a nonstick skillet over high heat until sizzling. Add the beef tenderloins and cook to your liking, then remove from the skillet and keep warm. Add the sour cream and mustard to the skillet and stir, then heat through. Season well with salt and pepper. Serve each beef tenderloin with a folded pancake and some sauce, scattered with a few snipped chives.

COOK'S NOTE

★ The pancakes can also make a vegetarian or nonmeat main course, stuffed with some creamed spinach or smoked fish and sour cream.

Apple & Date
Chutney

MAKES ONE 10½-OZ/300-G JAR

¾ cup cider vinegar
1 shallot, finely chopped
1 baking apple, peeled, cored,
   and chopped
¼ tsp ground allspice
10½ oz/300 g medjool dates,
   pitted and chopped
5 tbsp honey

✦ Put the vinegar, shallot, apple, and allspice in a saucepan and bring to a boil. Reduce the heat and simmer for 5 to 8 minutes. Add the dates and honey and cook for 8 to 10 minutes, until the dates are soft and the liquid is syrupy.

✦ Remove from the heat and let cool. Serve straight away or pack into sterilized jars and store in the refrigerator.

COOK'S NOTE

✦ Chutney makes a lovely Christmas gift. Simply tie a ribbon around the lid of the jar and add a decorative label with the date you made it—it will last for 6 weeks in the refrigerator.

Festive Jeweled
Rice

SERVES 6

1¼ cups basmati rice
⅓ cup red or wild rice
scant ½ cup plumped
   dried apricots
scant ¼ cup almonds, blanched
scant ¼ cup hazelnuts, toasted
1 fresh red chile, seeded and
   finely chopped
seeds of 1 pomegranate
1 tbsp finely chopped fresh parsley
1 tbsp finely chopped fresh mint
1 tbsp finely snipped fresh chives
2 tbsp white wine vinegar
6 tbsp extra virgin olive oil
1 shallot, finely chopped
salt and pepper

★ Cook the two types of rice separately according to the package directions. Drain and let cool, then tip into a large bowl.

★ Chop the apricots and nuts and add to the rice with the chile, pomegranate seeds, and the herbs. Mix together well.

★ Just before you are ready to serve, whisk the vinegar, oil, and shallot together in a pitcher and season well with salt and pepper. Pour the dressing over the rice and mix well. Pile into a serving dish.

COOK'S NOTE

★ You can use other dried fruits or nuts in this dish and exclude the chile if you prefer. Top with a few sliced salad onions for extra crunch.

Wild Mushroom

Filo Parcels

SERVES 6

¼ cup dried porcini mushrooms
5 tbsp butter
1 shallot, finely chopped
1 garlic clove, crushed
3½ oz/100 g cremini
    mushrooms, sliced
3½ oz/100 g button
    mushrooms, sliced
7 oz/200 g wild mushrooms,
    coarsely chopped
¾ cup basmati rice,
    cooked and cooled
2 tbsp dry sherry
1 tbsp soy sauce or
    mushroom sauce
1 tbsp chopped fresh
    flat-leaf parsley
18 sheets filo dough,
    thawed if frozen
vegetable oil, for oiling
1½ cups sour cream
¼ cup Madeira
salt and pepper

★ Put the dried mushrooms in a heatproof bowl and just cover with boiling water. Let soak for 20 minutes.

★ Meanwhile, melt half the butter in a large skillet over low heat. Add the shallot and garlic, then cook, stirring occasionally, for 5 to 8 minutes, until the shallot is transparent and soft. Add all the fresh mushrooms and cook, stirring, for 2 to 3 minutes.

★ Preheat the oven to 400°F/200°C. Drain the dried mushrooms, reserving the soaking liquid, and coarsely chop, then add to the skillet with the rice, sherry, soy sauce, and parsley. Season well with salt and pepper, then mix together well and simmer until most of the liquid has evaporated.

★ Melt the remaining butter in a small saucepan. Lay 1 sheet of filo dough on a counter and brush with melted butter. Put another sheet on top and brush with butter, then top with a third sheet. Spoon some of the mushroom mixture into the center, then fold in the edges to form a parcel. Use a little more of the melted butter to make sure that the edges are secure. Repeat to make 6 parcels.

★ Place the parcels on a lightly oiled baking sheet and brush with the remaining melted butter. Bake in the preheated oven for 25 to 30 minutes, until golden.

★ Meanwhile, to make the sauce, heat the reserved soaking liquid in a saucepan. Add the sour cream and Madeira, then stir over low heat until heated through. Season with salt and pepper to taste and serve with the parcels.

Parsnip & Potato
Cakes

SERVES 6

2 large potatoes
2 parsnips
olive oil, goose fat, or lard,
   for frying
salt and pepper

★ Peel and grate the potatoes and parsnips onto a clean dish towel. Squeeze out any excess liquid, then spread out onto another clean dish towel or paper towel and let stand for 10 minutes.

★ Put the potatoes and parsnips in a bowl, then mix together and season with salt and pepper to taste. Heat a little oil in a nonstick skillet over medium-high heat. Add a spoonful of the potato mixture, then flatten with the back of a spoon to form a cake and cook for 3 to 5 minutes, until brown and crisp. Carefully turn over and cook for an additional 2 to 3 minutes. Remove and drain on paper towels. Keep warm while you cook the remaining parsnip and potato mixture.

COOK'S NOTE

★ These cakes are also delicious for breakfast with a poached egg and some broiled pancetta, or with smoked salmon and sour cream and chives.

Perfect Roast
Potatoes

SERVES 8

5 tbsp goose or duck fat
   or 5 tbsp olive oil
2 lb 4 oz/1 kg even-size potatoes,
   peeled
coarse sea salt
8 fresh rosemary sprigs,
   for garnishing

★ Preheat the oven to 450°F/230°C. Put the fat in a large roasting pan, then sprinkle generously with sea salt and place in the oven.

★ Meanwhile, cook the potatoes in a large saucepan of boiling water for 8 to 10 minutes, until parboiled. Drain well and, if the potatoes are large, cut them in half. Return the potatoes to the empty saucepan and shake vigorously to roughen their outsides.

★ Arrange the potatoes in a single layer in the hot fat and roast for 45 minutes. If they look as if they are beginning to char around the edges, reduce the oven temperature to 400°F/200°C. Turn the potatoes over and roast for an additional 30 minutes, until crisp. Serve garnished with rosemary sprigs.

COOK'S NOTE
★ Use starchy potatoes, such as Yukon Gold for roasting, because these have the best texture. Do not let them stand around once they are cooked, or the outsides will turn leathery instead of crisp.

Two-Potato
Purée

SERVES 6

2 large orange sweet potatoes
½ tsp vegetable oil
4 potatoes
2 tbsp butter
½ cup heavy cream
whole nutmeg, for grating
salt and pepper

⭐ Preheat the oven to 375°F/190°C. Rub the sweet potatoes with the oil, then bake in the preheated oven for 20 to 25 minutes, until tender.

⭐ Meanwhile, peel the potatoes, then cook in a large saucepan of boiling water until tender. Drain well and put in a colander. Cover with a clean dish towel to absorb the steam and let stand until cooled. Mash the potatoes or pass through a potato ricer.

⭐ Scoop out the flesh from the sweet potatoes and mix well with the potato in a warmed bowl. Discard the sweet potato skins. Melt the butter with the cream in a small saucepan, then pour half over the potato mixture and beat well with a wooden spoon. Add the remaining cream mixture a little at a time until you achieve the consistency you like. Season with salt and pepper to taste, and add a grating of nutmeg. Beat again, then serve.

COOK'S NOTE

⭐ If you make the purée in advance, it can be put into a greased gratin dish and dotted with a little extra butter, then cooked under the broiler or in a low oven until golden on top.

Garlic Mushrooms with

White Wine

& Chestnuts

SERVES 4

4 tbsp butter
4 garlic cloves, chopped
7 oz/200 g button mushrooms,
   sliced
7 oz/200 g cremini mushrooms,
   sliced
4 tbsp dry white wine
heaping 1/3 cup heavy cream
10 1/2 oz/300 g canned whole
   chestnuts, drained
3 1/2 oz/100 g chanterelle
   mushrooms, sliced
salt and pepper
chopped fresh parsley, for
   garnishing

★ Melt the butter in a large saucepan over medium heat. Add the garlic and cook, stirring, for 3 minutes, until softened. Add the button and cremini mushrooms and cook for 3 minutes.

★ Stir in the wine and cream and season with salt and pepper to taste. Cook for 2 minutes, stirring, then add the chestnuts and the chanterelle mushrooms. Cook for an additional 2 minutes, stirring, then remove from the heat and transfer to a warmed serving dish. Garnish with chopped fresh parsley and serve.

COOK'S NOTE

★ Using three different types of mushrooms enhances both the flavor and texture of this dish. Button mushrooms are very mild, but readily absorb other flavors, such as garlic and wine. Cremini mushrooms are meatier and have a stronger flavor, while chanterelles are delicate in both texture and flavor.

Brussels Sprouts with
Buttered Chestnuts

SERVES 4

12 oz/350 g Brussels sprouts,
    trimmed
3 tbsp butter
3½ oz/100 g canned whole
    chestnuts
pinch of grated nutmeg
salt and pepper
½ cup slivered almonds,
    for garnishing

★ Bring a large saucepan of salted water to a boil. Add the Brussels sprouts and cook for 5 minutes. Drain thoroughly.

★ Melt the butter in a large saucepan over medium heat. Add the Brussels sprouts and cook, stirring, for 3 minutes, then add the chestnuts and nutmeg. Season with salt and pepper to taste and stir well. Cook for an additional 2 minutes, stirring, then remove from the heat. Transfer to a warmed serving dish, then scatter over the almonds and serve.

COOK'S NOTE

★ The slivered almonds in this dish add a lovely nutty flavor to the Brussels sprouts, which are superbly complemented by the chestnuts. When buying Brussels sprouts, look for tight buds with bright green-colored leaves and no sign of yellowing or sliminess. Choose sprouts that are about the same size for even cooking.

Sugar-Glazed
Parsnips

SERVES 8

24 small parsnips, peeled
about 1 tsp salt
8 tbsp butter
½ cup brown sugar

★ Place the parsnips in a saucepan and add just enough water to cover, then add the salt. Bring to a boil. Reduce the heat, then cover and simmer for 20 to 25 minutes, until tender. Drain well.

★ Melt the butter in a heavy-bottom skillet or wok. Add the parsnips and toss well. Sprinkle with the sugar, then cook, stirring frequently to prevent the sugar from sticking to the skillet or burning. Cook the parsnips for 10 to 15 minutes, until golden and glazed. Transfer to a warmed serving dish and serve immediately.

COOK'S NOTE

★ When buying parsnips, look for firm roots with no rusty patches and no damage to the skin. Store them in a cool, well-ventilated place for up to 5 days. Try to buy parsnips that are all about the same size, for even cooking.

Glazed Red Cabbage with
Golden Raisins

SERVES 4

2 tbsp butter
1 garlic clove, chopped
1½ lb/650 g red cabbage, shredded
scant 1 cup golden raisins
1 tbsp honey
⅓ cup red wine
⅓ cup water

★ Melt the butter in a large saucepan over medium heat. Add the garlic and cook, stirring, for 1 minute, until slightly softened.

★ Add the cabbage and golden raisins, then stir in the honey. Cook for an additional minute. Pour in the wine and water and bring to a boil. Reduce the heat, then cover and simmer gently, stirring occasionally, for 45 minutes, until the cabbage is cooked. Serve hot.

COOK'S NOTE

★ Red cabbage is a classic accompaniment to game, such as pheasant, and roast pork or ham. It also goes well with some poultry, notably goose and duck, counteracting the richness of the meat.

Spiced Winter *Vegetables*

SERVES 4

4 parsnips, scrubbed and
   trimmed but left unpeeled
4 carrots, scrubbed and
   trimmed but left unpeeled
2 onions, quartered
1 red onion, quartered
3 leeks, trimmed and cut
   into 2½-inch/6-cm slices
6 garlic cloves, left unpeeled
   and whole
6 tbsp extra virgin olive oil
½ tsp mild chili powder
pinch of paprika
salt and pepper

★ Preheat the oven to 425°F/220°C. Bring a large saucepan of water to a boil.

★ Cut the parsnips and carrots into wedges of similar size. Add them to the saucepan and cook for 5 minutes. Drain thoroughly and place in an ovenproof dish with the onions, leeks, and garlic. Pour over the oil and sprinkle in the spices and salt and pepper to taste, then mix until all the vegetables are well coated.

★ Roast in the preheated oven for at least 1 hour. Turn the vegetables from time to time until they are tender and starting to color. Remove from the oven and transfer to a warmed serving dish, then serve immediately.

COOK'S NOTE

★ Providing there is room in the oven, these vegetables are ideal for Christmas lunch, because they offer a selection of different flavors without taking up the entire stove and several saucepans.

Pork, Cranberry, & *Herb Stuffing*

SERVES 6

1 tbsp vegetable oil, plus extra
   for oiling
1 onion, finely chopped
2 celery stalks, chopped
1 lb/450 g pork sausage meat
1 cup fresh white or whole wheat
   breadcrumbs
½ cup dried cranberries
¾ cup fresh cranberries
1 tbsp chopped fresh parsley
1 tbsp chopped fresh sage
1 tbsp chopped fresh thyme leaves
1 large egg, beaten
salt and pepper

✷ Heat the oil in a heavy-bottom skillet over medium heat. Add the onion and celery, then cook, stirring frequently, for 10 minutes, until the onion is transparent and soft.

✷ Meanwhile, preheat the oven to 375°F/190°C. Break up the sausage meat in a large bowl. Add the breadcrumbs, dried and fresh cranberries, and the herbs and mix together well. Add the cooked onion and celery, then the egg. Season well with salt and pepper and mix together thoroughly.

✷ Form the stuffing into balls, then place on an oiled baking sheet and bake in the preheated oven for 25 minutes. Alternatively, spoon into 2 foil pans, level the surface, then bake for 45 minutes.

COOK'S NOTE

✷ This stuffing can be made in advance and frozen, as long as the sausage meat has not previously been frozen. Thaw thoroughly before cooking.

Chestnut & Sausage

Stuffing

SERVES 6–8

8 oz/225 g pork sausage meat
8 oz/225 g unsweetened
   chestnut purée
¾ cup walnuts, chopped
⅔ cup plumped dried apricots,
   chopped
2 tbsp chopped fresh parsley
2 tbsp snipped fresh chives
2 tsp chopped fresh sage
4–5 tbsp heavy cream
salt and pepper

★ Combine the sausage meat and chestnut purée in a bowl, then stir in the walnuts, apricots, parsley, chives, and sage. Stir in enough cream to make a firm, but not dry, mixture. Season with salt and pepper to taste.

★ If you are planning to stuff a turkey or goose, fill the neck cavity only to ensure the bird cooks all the way through. It is safer and more reliable to cook the stuffing separately, either rolled into small balls and placed on a baking sheet or spooned into an ovenproof dish.

★ Cook the separate stuffing in a preheated oven for 30 to 40 minutes at 375°F/190°C. It should be allowed a longer time to cook if you are roasting a bird at a lower temperature in the same oven.

COOK'S NOTE

★ The combination of nuts, fruit, and herbs in this stuffing helps to counteract the richness of traditional Christmas poultry, such as turkey and goose. It also produces an appetizing aroma during cooking.

Cranberry

Sauce

SERVES 8

thinly pared rind and juice
  of 1 lemon
thinly pared rind and juice
  of 1 orange
scant 3³/₄ cups cranberries,
  thawed if frozen
³/₄ cup superfine sugar
2 tbsp arrowroot, mixed
  with 3 tbsp cold water

★ Cut the strips of lemon and orange rind into thin shreds and place in a heavy-bottom saucepan. If using fresh cranberries, rinse well and remove any stalks. Add the berries, citrus juice, and sugar to the saucepan and cook over medium heat, stirring occasionally, for 5 minutes, or until the berries begin to burst.

★ Strain the juice into a clean saucepan and set the cranberries aside. Stir the arrowroot mixture into the juice, then bring to a boil, stirring continuously, until the sauce is smooth and thickened. Remove from the heat and stir in the reserved cranberries.

★ Transfer the cranberry sauce to a bowl and let cool, then cover with plastic wrap and chill in the refrigerator.

COOK'S NOTE

★ Turkey and cranberry sauce make a classic Christmas partnership. However, cranberry sauce can also be served to good effect with game, roast duck, or chicken, or even some oily fish.

Pickled Apricots with

Star Anise

**MAKES TWO
1 LB 2-OZ/500-G JARS**

2 cups cider vinegar
1 lb 2 oz/500 g unrefined
    superfine sugar
1 lb 2 oz/500 g plumped
    dried apricots
2 dried chiles
4 star anise

★ Heat the vinegar and sugar in a saucepan over medium heat, stirring until all the sugar has dissolved. Add the apricots, chiles, and star anise to the saucepan and bring to a boil. Reduce the heat and simmer for 15 minutes, until the syrup has thickened.

★ Ladle the apricots into sterilized jars and cover with the syrup. Let cool, then seal the jars and store in a dark, cool place for up to 2 weeks.

COOK'S NOTE

★ The apricots can be packed into smaller jars to give as gifts—place an extra star anise in each jar against the glass for a decorative effect.

Party Food &
Drinks

Cranberry

Vodka

MAKES 3 CUPS

**heaping 2 cups fresh
  cranberries**
⅓ cup superfine sugar
3 cups vodka
**¼ cup Cointreau
  (optional)**

FOR SERVING
frozen cranberries
orange or mandarin rind

★ Put the cranberries and sugar in a sterilized 1-quart/1-liter jar and crush the fruit until the juice runs. Add the vodka (keep the empty vodka bottle) and stir, then seal the jar. Store in a cool, dark place for 6 weeks, giving the jar a shake every now and again.

★ Strain the vodka back into its original bottle (which must be sterilized) or into a pitcher, then stir in the Cointreau, if using. To serve, place some frozen cranberries in a chilled Martini glass and add a twist of orange or mandarin rind, then pour over the cranberry vodka.

COOK'S NOTE

★ This is also delicious poured over sherbet as a refreshing dessert—try it over raspberry or strawberry sherbet.

Hot Rum

Punch

MAKES 4½ QUARTS/4.3 LITERS

3½ cups rum
3½ cups brandy
2½ cups freshly squeezed lemon
   juice
3–4 tbsp superfine sugar
8½ cups boiling water
slices of fruit, for decorating

 Mix together the rum, brandy, lemon juice, and 3 tablespoons of the sugar in a punch bowl or large heatproof mixing bowl. Pour in the boiling water and stir well to mix. Taste and add more sugar if required. Decorate with the fruit slices and serve immediately in heatproof glasses with handles.

COOK'S NOTE

 This warming drink is a great way to greet guests on Christmas evening and a much-deserved reward for those who venture out for a brisk walk on Boxing Day. Santa Claus probably deserves a glass, too.

Mulled Ale &
Mulled Wine

MULLED ALE
MAKES 3 QUARTS/2.8 LITERS

scant 2¾ quarts strong ale
1¼ cups brandy
2 tbsp superfine sugar
large pinch of ground cloves
large pinch of ground ginger

MULLED WINE
MAKES 3½ QUARTS/3.3 LITERS

5 oranges
50 cloves
thinly pared rind and juice
    of 4 lemons
3½ cups water
½ cup superfine sugar
2 cinnamon sticks
8½ cups red wine
⅔ cup brandy

Mulled Ale

★ Put all the ingredients in a heavy-bottom saucepan and heat gently, stirring, until the sugar has dissolved. Continue to heat so that it is simmering but not boiling. Remove the saucepan from the heat and serve the ale immediately in heatproof glasses.

Mulled Wine

★ Prick the skins of 3 of the oranges all over with a fork and stud with the cloves, then set aside. Thinly pare the rind and squeeze the juice from the remaining oranges.

★ Put the orange rind and juice, lemon rind and juice, water, sugar, and cinnamon in a heavy-bottom saucepan and bring to a boil over medium heat, stirring occasionally, until the sugar has dissolved. Boil for 2 minutes without stirring, then remove from the heat. Stir once and let stand for 10 minutes. Strain the liquid into a heatproof pitcher, pressing down on the contents of the strainer to extract all the juice.

★ Pour the wine into a separate saucepan and add the strained spiced juices, the brandy, and the clove-studded oranges. Simmer gently without boiling, then remove the saucepan from the heat. Strain into heatproof glasses and serve the mulled wine immediately.

Cheese *Straws*

MAKES 10–12

8 tbsp unsalted butter, plus extra
    for greasing
scant 1 cup all-purpose flour, plus
    extra for dusting
pinch of salt
pinch of paprika
1 tsp mustard powder
3 oz/85 g cheddar or Gruyère
    cheese, grated
1 egg, lightly beaten
1–2 tbsp cold water
poppy seeds, for coating

★ Preheat the oven to 400°F/200°C. Lightly grease 2 baking sheets with butter.

★ Sift the flour, salt, paprika, and mustard powder into a bowl. Add the remaining butter and cut it into the flour with a knife, then rub in with your fingertips until the mixture resembles breadcrumbs. Stir in the cheese and add half of the beaten egg, then mix in enough water to make a firm dough. The dough may be stored in the freezer. Thaw at room temperature before rolling out.

★ Spread out the poppy seeds on a plate. Turn the dough onto a lightly floured counter and knead briefly, then roll out. Using a sharp knife, cut into strips measuring 4 x ¼ inches/10 x 0.5 cm. Brush with the remaining beaten egg and roll the straws in the poppy seeds to coat, then arrange them on the baking sheets. Gather up the dough trimmings and reroll. Stamp out 10–12 rounds with a 2½-inch/6-cm fluted cutter, then stamp out the centers with a 2-inch/5-cm plain cutter. Brush with the egg and place on the baking sheets.

★ Bake in the preheated oven for 10 minutes, until golden brown. Set aside the cheese straws on the baking sheets to cool slightly, then transfer to cooling racks to cool completely. Store in an airtight container. Thread the pastry straws through the pastry rings before serving.

COOK'S NOTE

★ Rather than using poppy seeds, you can brush the cheese straws with mild mustard and sprinkle with a little cayenne pepper before baking. Be careful not to make them too spicy.

Scallops Wrapped
in Pancetta

MAKES 12

12 fresh rosemary sprigs
6 raw scallops, corals removed
12 thin-cut pancetta slices

DRESSING
2 tbsp olive oil
1 tbsp white wine vinegar
1 tsp honey
salt and pepper

★ First prepare the rosemary by stripping most of the leaves off the stalks, leaving a cluster of leaves at the top. Trim the stalks to about 2½ inches/6 cm long, cutting each tip at the base end at an angle.

★ Cut each scallop in half through the center to give 2 disks of scallop, then wrap each one in a pancetta slice and, keeping the end tucked under, place on a plate. Cover and chill in the refrigerator for 15 minutes.

★ To make the dressing, whisk the oil, vinegar, and honey together in a small bowl and season with salt and pepper to taste.

★ Preheat the broiler to high or heat a ridged grill pan over high heat. Cook the scallops under the broiler or on the grill pan for 2 minutes on each side, until the pancetta is crisp and brown. Spear each one on a prepared rosemary skewer and serve hot, with the dressing as a dip.

COOK'S NOTE

★ These could be served alongside cocktail sausages and angels on horseback (oysters wrapped in pancetta) as delicious hot party snacks.

Piquant Crab *Bites*

MAKES 50

2 cups fresh white breadcrumbs
2 large eggs, separated
scant 1 cup sour cream
1 tsp mustard powder
1 lb 2 oz/500 g fresh
    white crabmeat
1 tbsp chopped fresh dill
peanut oil, for frying
salt and pepper
2 limes, quartered, for serving

★ Tip the breadcrumbs into a large bowl. In a separate bowl, whisk the egg yolks with the sour cream and mustard powder and add to the breadcrumbs with the crabmeat and dill. Season with salt and pepper to taste, then mix together well. Cover and chill in the refrigerator for 15 minutes.

★ In a clean bowl, whisk the egg whites until stiff. Lightly fold a tablespoonful of the egg whites into the crab mixture, then fold in the remaining egg whites.

★ Heat 2 tablespoons of oil in a nonstick skillet over medium-high heat. Drop in as many teaspoonfuls of the crab mixture as will fit in the skillet without overcrowding, then flatten slightly and cook for 2 minutes, until brown and crisp. Flip over and cook for an additional 1 to 2 minutes, until the undersides are browned. Remove and drain on paper towels. Keep warm while you cook the remaining crab mixture, adding more oil to the skillet if necessary.

★ Serve the crab bites warm with the lime quarters for squeezing over.

COOK'S NOTE

★ These can be made in advance and reheated in a medium oven. They also freeze well, in which case they should be cooked, cooled, and then frozen. Thaw thoroughly before reheating.

Leek & Bacon
Tartlets

MAKES 12

PIE DOUGH
7 tbsp unsalted butter, chilled and diced, plus extra for greasing
scant 1¾ cups all-purpose flour
pinch of salt
½ tsp paprika

FILLING
2 tbsp unsalted butter
1 tsp olive oil
1 leek, trimmed and chopped
8 unsmoked bacon slices, cut into small pieces
2 eggs, beaten
⅔ cup heavy cream
1 tsp snipped fresh chives
salt and pepper

★ Lightly grease a 3-inch/7.5-cm, 12-cup muffin pan with butter. Sift the flour, salt, and paprika into a bowl and rub in the remaining butter until the mixture resembles breadcrumbs. Add a very little cold water—just enough to bring the dough together. Knead the dough briefly on a floured counter.

★ Divide the dough in half. Roll out 1 piece of dough and, using a 3½-inch/9-cm plain cutter, cut out 6 rounds, then roll each round into a 4½-inch/12-cm round. Repeat with the other half of the dough until you have 12 rounds, then use to line the muffin pan. Cover and chill in the refrigerator for 30 minutes.

★ Meanwhile, preheat the oven to 400°F/200°C. To make the filling, melt the butter with the oil in a nonstick skillet over medium heat, then add the leek and cook, stirring frequently, for 5 minutes until soft. Remove with a slotted spoon and set aside. Add the bacon pieces to the skillet and cook for 5 minutes, until crisp. Remove and drain on paper towels.

★ Line the pastry shells with parchment paper and dried beans and bake in the preheated oven for 10 minutes. Whisk the eggs and cream together in a bowl and season with salt and pepper to taste, then stir in the chives with the cooked leek and bacon. Remove the pastry shells from the oven and carefully lift out the paper and beans. Divide the bacon and leek mixture among the pastry shells and bake for 10 minutes, until the tarts are golden and risen. Let cool in the pan for 5 minutes, then carefully transfer to a cooling rack. Serve warm or cold.

Corn & Parmesan

Fritters

MAKES 25-30

5 fresh corn on the cob
   or 1 lb 2 oz/500 g frozen or
   canned corn kernels
2 eggs, beaten
4 tbsp all-purpose flour
2 tbsp finely grated
   Parmesan cheese
1 tsp baking soda
4 tbsp whole milk
vegetable oil, for frying
salt

★ If you are using fresh corn on the cobs, cook them in a large saucepan of boiling water for 7 minutes, then drain well. Stand them on their ends, then cut away the kernels and let cool. If using frozen corn kernels, set aside to thaw first, or drain canned corn kernels.

★ Put the corn kernels in a bowl with the eggs, flour, Parmesan cheese, baking soda, and a pinch of salt. Mix together, then add the milk and stir together well.

★ Pour oil into a deep saucepan to a depth of 1½ inches/4 cm, then heat it to a temperature of 350–375°F/180–190°C, or until a cube of bread browns in 30 seconds. Drop 4 teaspoonfuls of the mixture into the oil at a time and cook for 2 minutes. Turn over and cook for an additional minute or so, until crisp, brown, and slightly puffed up. Remove and drain on paper towels. Keep warm while you cook the remaining batches of mixture—you may need to add a little more oil between batches and scoop out any stray corn kernels. Sprinkle with salt to serve.

COOK'S NOTE

★ You could replace the Parmesan cheese with ½ teaspoon of either paprika or chili powder for extra bite.

Smoked Turkey &

Stuffing Parcels

MAKES 12

12 slices smoked turkey breast
4 tbsp cranberry sauce
14 oz/400 g cooked and cooled
   sausage meat stuffing
24 sheets filo dough, thawed
   if frozen
5 tbsp butter, melted

★ Preheat the oven to 375°F/190°C. Put a nonstick baking sheet into the oven to heat.

★ For each parcel, spread a slice of smoked turkey with a teaspoonful of cranberry sauce and spoon 1¼ oz/35 g of the stuffing into the center, then roll up the turkey slice. Lay 1 sheet of filo dough on a counter and brush with a little of the melted butter. Put another sheet on top, then put the rolled-up turkey in the center. Add a little more cranberry sauce, then carefully fold the filo dough around the turkey, tucking under the ends to form a neat parcel. Repeat to make 12 parcels.

★ Place the parcels on the hot baking sheet and brush with the remaining melted butter, then bake in the preheated oven for 25 minutes, until golden. Serve hot.

COOK'S NOTE

★ You can add a few chopped chestnuts or other Christmas leftovers to these parcels, or replace the turkey with cooked chicken.

Desserts &

After-Dinner Treats

Gingered Brandy *Snaps*

MAKES 36

vegetable oil, for oiling
8 tbsp unsalted butter
scant ½ cup dark corn syrup
½ cup raw brown sugar
scant 1 cup all-purpose flour
2 tsp ground ginger
2½ cups stiffly whipped heavy
 cream, for serving

★ Preheat the oven to 325°F/160°C. Brush a nonstick baking sheet with oil. Place the butter, syrup, and sugar in a saucepan and set over low heat, stirring occasionally, until melted and combined. Remove the saucepan from the heat and let cool slightly. Sift the flour and ground ginger together into the butter mixture and beat until smooth. Spoon 2 teaspoons of the mixture onto the baking sheet, spacing them well apart. Bake for 8 minutes, until pale golden brown. Keep the remaining mixture warm. Meanwhile, oil the handle of a wooden spoon.

★ Remove the baking sheet from the oven and let stand for 1 minute so that the brandy snaps firm up slightly. Remove 1 with a palette knife and immediately curl it around the handle of the wooden spoon. Once set, carefully slide it off the handle and transfer to a cooling rack to cool completely. Repeat with the other brandy snap. Bake the remaining mixture and shape in the same way, using a cool baking sheet each time. Do not be tempted to cook more, or the rounds will set before you have time to shape them. When all the brandy snaps are cool, store in an airtight container.

★ To serve, spoon the whipped cream into a pastry bag fitted with a star tip. Fill the brandy snaps with cream from both ends.

COOK'S NOTE

★ The unfilled brandy snaps will keep for at least a week in an airtight container. Do not fill them with cream until you are almost ready to serve, or they will become soggy and collapse as guests try to eat them.

Festive Sherry
Dessert

SERVES 4-6

3½ oz/100 g sponge cake
raspberry preserve, for spreading
⅔ cup sherry
heaping ½ cup frozen raspberries,
    thawed
scant 2½ cups fresh strawberries,
    sliced

CUSTARD LAYER
6 egg yolks
¼ cup superfine sugar
2 cups milk
1 tsp vanilla extract

TOPPING
1¼ cups heavy cream
1-2 tbsp superfine sugar
1 chocolate bar, crumbled

★ Spread the sponge cake with preserve, then cut into bite-size cubes and arrange them in the bottom of a large glass serving bowl. Pour over the sherry and let stand for 30 minutes.

★ Combine the raspberries and strawberries and spoon them over the cake pieces in the bowl.

★ To make the custard, put the egg yolks and sugar into a bowl and whisk together. Pour the milk into a saucepan and warm gently over low heat. Remove from the heat and gradually stir into the egg mixture, then return the mixture to the saucepan and stir continuously over low heat until thickened. Do not boil. Remove from the heat, then pour into a bowl and stir in the vanilla. Let cool for 1 hour. Spread the custard over the dessert, cover with plastic wrap, and chill in the refrigerator for 2 hours.

★ To make the topping, whip the cream in a bowl and stir in the sugar to taste. Spread the cream over the dessert, and then scatter over the chocolate pieces. Chill in the refrigerator for 30 minutes before serving.

COOK'S NOTE

★ Fresh strawberries may not be widely available at Christmas and, in any case, are likely to be quite expensive. As an alternative, crumble 12 almond macaroons or amaretti cookies over the cake pieces and then spoon the raspberries on top, omitting the strawberries altogether.

Cinnamon Poached Fruits
with Cookies

SERVES 6

scant ¾ cup plumped
    dried apricots
scant ¾ cup dried figs, halved
5½ oz/150 g medjool dates,
    pitted and halved lengthwise
scant ¾ cup golden raisins
2 cinnamon sticks
2 star anise
5 cardamom pods, crushed
1 tbsp water
2 cups Beaumes de Venise or
    other dessert wine
marscapone cheese or sour
    cream, for serving
seeds from 1 pomegranate,
    for decorating

ALMOND COOKIES
1⅓ cups ground almonds
scant 1 cup superfine sugar
3 tbsp finely grated orange rind
⅓ cup all-purpose flour
3 large egg whites
½ cup slivered almonds, toasted
2 tbsp white confectioners' sugar

★ The day before you want to serve, put all the fruit in a saucepan with the cinnamon sticks, star anise, and cardamom pods. Add the water and wine, then heat very gently to a simmer and poach for 5 minutes. Remove from the heat and remove the cardamom pods and star anise, but leave in the cinnamon sticks. Let cool completely, then cover and chill overnight in the refrigerator.

★ Preheat the oven to 350°F/180°C. Line 2 baking sheets with parchment paper.

★ To make the cookies, put the ground almonds in a bowl and add ½ cup of the superfine sugar, the orange rind, and flour, then stir well. In a separate bowl, whisk the egg whites until they form soft peaks, then whisk in the remaining superfine sugar until the mixture is glossy and stiff. Fold the egg whites into the almond mixture.

★ Place teaspoonfuls of the dough, spaced well apart, on the baking sheets, then sprinkle over the almonds. Bake in the preheated oven for 12 minutes, until puffed up and beginning to brown. Dust with the confectioners' sugar and let cool for 10 minutes before transferring to a cooling rack to cool completely.

★ To serve, remove the cinnamon sticks from the poached fruit and divide among 6 stemmed glasses. Spoon over a little mascarpone cheese and scatter over the pomegranate seeds. Serve with the almond cookies.

Berry Compôte
with Cassis

SERVES 6

scant 3 cups raspberries
scant 3¼ cups black currants
scant ½ cup superfine sugar
²/₃ cup water
2 tbsp arrowroot, mixed with a little cold water
2 tbsp crème de cassis
heavy cream, for serving

★ Put the raspberries, black currants, sugar, and water in a heavy-bottom saucepan. Cover and cook over low heat for 15 minutes, until the fruit is soft.

★ Put the arrowroot mixture in a separate saucepan. Bring to a boil, stirring continuously, until thickened. Remove from the heat and let cool slightly, then stir in the black currants, raspberries, and crème de cassis.

★ Pour the compôte into a glass bowl and let cool. Cover and chill in the refrigerator for at least 1 hour. To serve, divide the compôte among 6 decorative glass dishes and top with a swirl of cream.

COOK'S NOTE

★ This is a quick and easy alternative to Christmas pudding that will be welcomed by those watching their waistlines. It is also a good choice for a Boxing Day lunch, when people appreciate a change of flavors and some lighter dishes.

Chocolate Chestnut

Roulade

SERVES 6

6 large eggs, separated
¾ cup superfine sugar
½ tsp vanilla or chocolate extract
½ cup unsweetened cocoa
confectioners' sugar, for dusting
1 cup heavy cream
9 oz/250 g sweetened
   chestnut purée
2 tbsp brandy
2½ oz/70 g cooked peeled
   chestnuts, chopped

★ Preheat the oven to 350°F/180°C. Line a 9 x 17¾-inch/23 x 45-cm jelly roll pan with parchment paper.

★ Using an electric whisk, beat the egg yolks, superfine sugar, and vanilla extract together in a bowl for 10 minutes, until doubled in volume and pale and fluffy. In a separate bowl, whisk the egg whites until they form soft peaks. Fold a tablespoonful of egg whites into the egg yolk mixture, then gently fold in the remaining egg whites and the unsweetened cocoa.

★ Spoon the cake batter into the prepared pan and level the surface with a palette knife. Bake in the preheated oven for 20 minutes, until risen. Let cool in the pan.

★ Put a large piece of parchment paper over a clean dish towel and dust with confectioners' sugar. Invert the sponge onto the parchment paper and carefully peel away the lining paper. In a clean bowl, whisk the cream until stiff, then stir in the chestnut purée and the brandy. Spread over the sponge, leaving a 1-inch/2.5-cm margin around the edges, and scatter over the chestnuts. Using one end of the dish towel, careful roll up the roulade. Dust with more confectioners' sugar.

COOK'S NOTE

★ You could replace the chestnuts in the filling with chopped semisweet chocolate or a few raspberries, if you like.

Orange Ice Cream with
Almond Praline

SERVES 6

1 large orange, sliced
½ cup granulated sugar
¾ cup water
½ tsp orange flower water
butter, for greasing
heaping 1 cup superfine sugar
1¼ cups slivered almonds, toasted

ICE CREAM
1 vanilla bean
1¼ cups light cream
4 large egg yolks
2 tsp custard powder
¼ cup superfine sugar
1¼ cups sour cream

⭐ Cut away the flesh of the orange, leaving the rind and a little pith. Cut the rind into 2-inch/5-cm pieces. Put the granulated sugar and ⅓ cup of the water in a saucepan and heat gently, stirring, until the sugar has dissolved. Bring to a boil and add the orange flower water and orange rind. Reduce the heat and simmer gently for 15 to 20 minutes. Let the rind cool slightly in the syrup, then lift out onto wax paper to cool completely, and then coarsely chop.

⭐ Grease a piece of foil with butter. Put the sugar in a saucepan with the remaining water and heat gently, stirring, until the sugar has dissolved. Bring to a simmer, swirling the saucepan, and cook until the syrup reaches a caramel-orange color. Remove from the heat and add the almonds. Stir, then pour onto the greased foil and spread out. Let cool and harden, then break into shards.

⭐ To make the ice cream, slit the vanilla bean open and scrape out the seeds. Put the bean and cream in a saucepan and heat gently. Put the vanilla seeds, egg yolks, custard powder, and sugar in a heatproof bowl and whisk until smooth. When the cream is about to boil, remove the vanilla bean and, whisking continuously, pour the cream over the egg yolk mixture. Continuing to stir, pour the mixture into the saucepan and bring to a boil. Reduce the heat and simmer until thickened. Plunge the saucepan's bottom into a bowl of iced water, then stir until cool. Fold in the sour cream and orange peel. When cold, pour into an ice-cream machine and churn according to the manufacturer's directions. Alternatively, pour into a freezerproof container and cover, then freeze for 12 hours. Remove from the freezer and beat to break down any ice crystals. Refreeze and beat as before, then refreeze until solid. Serve with the praline.

Poached Pears
with Marsala

SERVES 6

6 Comice or other dessert pears,
   peeled but left whole with
   stalks attached
2 cups Marsala
½ cup water
1 tbsp brown sugar
1 piece of lemon rind or mandarin
   rind
1 vanilla bean
1½ cups cream
1 tbsp confectioners' sugar

★ Put the pears in a large saucepan with the Marsala, water, brown sugar, and lemon rind and bring gently to a boil, stirring to make sure that the sugar has dissolved. Reduce the heat, then cover and simmer for 30 minutes, until the pears are tender. Let the pears cool in the liquid. Remove the pears from the liquid, then cover and chill in the refrigerator.

★ Discard the lemon rind and let the liquid bubble for 15 to 20 minutes, until syrupy. Let cool.

★ Cut a thin sliver of flesh from the base of each pear so that they will stand upright. Slit the vanilla bean open and scrape out the seeds into a bowl. Whisk the cream, vanilla seeds, and confectioners' sugar together in a bowl until thick. Put each pear on a dessert plate and pour over a little syrup. Serve with the vanilla cream.

COOK'S NOTE

★ You can add a few pieces of chopped preserved ginger to the syrup when cool and serve the pears with some preserved ginger or cinnamon ice cream.

Roast Plums with

Armagnac Cream

SERVES 6

24 ripe plums
3½ tbsp unsalted butter,
    plus extra for greasing
2 tbsp maple syrup or
    flower honey
1¼ cups heavy cream
2 tbsp confectioners' sugar
2 large egg whites
2 tbsp Armagnac or brandy
finely grated rind of 1 lemon
1 tsp rose water (optional)

★ Preheat the oven to 400°F/200°C. Grease a baking sheet with butter.

★ Cut each plum in half and remove and discard the pit. Place cut-sides up on the prepared baking sheet, then dot each plum with some of the butter and drizzle over the maple syrup. Cover with foil. Bake in the preheated oven for 20 to 25 minutes, until tender. Let cool.

★ Whisk the cream in a bowl until beginning to thicken, adding a little sugar at a time. In a separate bowl, whisk the egg whites until stiff. Stir the Armagnac into the cream, then fold in the egg whites, followed by half the lemon rind.

★ To serve, divide the plum halves among 6 serving plates, then drizzle over the rose water, if using, and spoon over some of the Armagnac cream. Scatter over the remaining lemon rind and serve.

COOK'S NOTE

★ For a quick plate dessert, simply slice some pound cake or sponge cake onto a plate. Spoon over the roast plums and top with Armagnac cream, then scatter with a few toasted almonds.

Traditional Brandy
Butter

SERVES 6-8

**8 tbsp unsalted butter,
  at room temperature**
¼ cup superfine sugar
**½ cup confectioners' sugar,
  sifted**
3 tbsp brandy

★ Cream the butter in a bowl until it is very smooth and soft. Gradually beat in both types of sugar. Add the brandy, a little at a time, beating well after each addition and taking care not to let the mixture curdle.

★ Spread out the butter on a sheet of foil, then cover and chill in the refrigerator until firm. Keep chilled until ready to serve.

COOK'S NOTE

★ As an alternative, make a tasty rum butter. Beat the finely grated rind of 1 unwaxed orange into the butter with the two types of sugar and substitute dark or white rum for the brandy, adding it gradually to avoid curdling.

Chocolate Truffle *Selection*

MAKES 40-50

8 oz/225 g semisweet chocolate,
   minimum 70% cocoa solids
3/4 cup whipping cream
unsweetened cocoa, confectioners'
   sugar, or chopped toasted
   almonds, for coating

★ Coarsely chop the chocolate and put in a large heatproof bowl. Put the cream in a saucepan and bring up to boiling point. Pour over the chocolate and whisk until smooth. Let cool at room temperature for 1½ to 2 hours.

★ Cover 2 baking sheets with plastic wrap or parchment paper. Using a teaspoon, take bite-size scoops of the chocolate mixture and roll in unsweetened cocoa, confectioners' sugar, or chopped nuts to form balls, then place on the prepared baking sheets and chill in the refrigerator until set.

COOK'S NOTE

★ You can also add other flavors to the truffles—add a little brandy, Calvados, or dark rum to the mixture before you set it aside to set. The truffles could also be covered in milk chocolate or white chocolate—a mixture looks inviting when boxed as a gift.

Baked Alaska with *Soaked Fruits*

SERVES 4

7 oz/200 g luxury mixed dried
   fruit, plus extra for serving
¼ cup dark rum
1 homemade or prepared
   8-inch/20-cm sponge cake
heaping 2 cups vanilla ice cream
3 egg whites
scant 1 cup superfine sugar
½ tsp cream of tartar

★ The day before you want to serve, put the dried fruit (including extra for serving) and rum in a saucepan and heat gently for 5 minutes. Let cool, then cover and chill in the refrigerator overnight.

★ Preheat the oven to 425°F/220°C. Use the sponge cake to cover the base of an ovenproof serving dish. Pour boiling water into a pitcher and stand an ice-cream scoop in the hot water, then take the ice cream out of the freezer.

★ Whisk the egg whites in a large bowl until soft peaks form, then add the sugar a little at a time, whisking well between additions. Whisk in the cream of tartar and continue to whisk until the mixture is glossy and stiff.

★ Using a slotted spoon, transfer the fruit to the sponge cake base and spread out evenly, leaving a 2-inch/5-cm border around the edge. Using the hot, dried ice-cream scoop, quickly place scoops of the ice cream onto the fruit-topped sponge, with a couple of scoops on top to form a pyramid shape. Quickly spoon the meringue over the ice cream to cover it completely and up to the edge of the sponge cake.

★ Bake in the preheated oven for 7 minutes, until golden. Serve immediately with the extra rum-soaked fruit on the side.

COOK'S NOTE

★ You could replace the vanilla ice cream with rum raisin ice cream, or make a chocolate version with chocolate cake and chocolate ice cream.

Dark & White Chocolate

Florentines

MAKES 20

2 tbsp unsalted butter,
   plus extra for greasing
2 tbsp superfine flour, plus extra
   for dusting
⅓ cup superfine sugar
4 tbsp heavy cream
⅓ cup whole blanched almonds,
   coarsely chopped
½ cup slivered almonds, toasted
¼ cup candied peel, chopped
1¾ oz/50 g undyed candied
   cherries, chopped
1¾ oz/50 g preserved ginger,
   drained and chopped
2½ oz/70 g semisweet chocolate,
   minimum 70% cocoa solids,
   broken into pieces
2½ oz/70 g white chocolate,
   broken into pieces

★ Preheat the oven to 375°F/190°C. Lightly grease 2 baking sheets with butter and dust with flour, shaking to remove any excess.

★ Put the remaining butter and flour with the sugar in a small saucepan and heat gently, stirring well, until the mixture has melted. Gradually add the cream, stirring continuously, then add all the remaining ingredients, except the chocolate, and stir thoroughly. Remove from the heat and let cool.

★ Drop 5 teaspoonfuls of the dough onto each of the prepared baking sheets, spaced well apart to allow for spreading, then flatten with the back of a spoon. Bake in the preheated oven for 12 to 15 minutes. Let the cookies harden on the sheets for 2 to 3 minutes before transferring to a cooling rack. Repeat with the remaining dough, again using the 2 baking sheets.

★ When the cookies are completely cool, put the semisweet chocolate in a heatproof bowl, then set the bowl over a saucepan of barely simmering water and heat until melted. Using a teaspoon, spread the base of 10 of the cookies with the melted chocolate and place chocolate side-up on a cooling rack to set. Repeat with the white chocolate and the remaining 10 cookies.

COOK'S NOTE

★ Use whole candied peel if you can find it and chop it yourself. If you don't like ginger, replace it with angelica or dyed green cherries.

Tuscan Christmas *Cake*

SERVES 12-14

¾ cup hazelnuts
¾ cup almonds
½ cup candied peel
⅓ cup plumped dried apricots,
 finely chopped
⅓ cup candied pineapple,
 finely chopped
grated rind of 1 orange
heaping ⅓ cup all-purpose flour
2 tbsp unsweetened cocoa
1 tsp ground cinnamon
¼ tsp ground coriander
¼ tsp freshly grated nutmeg
¼ tsp ground cloves
½ cup superfine sugar
½ cup honey
confectioners' sugar,
 for decorating

★ Preheat the oven to 350°F/180°C. Line the cake pan with parchment paper. Spread out the hazelnuts on a baking sheet and toast in the oven for 10 minutes, until golden brown. Tip them onto a dish towel and rub off the skins.

★ Meanwhile, spread out the almonds on a baking sheet and toast in the oven for 10 minutes until golden. Watch carefully after 7 minutes, as they can burn easily. Reduce the oven temperature to 300°F/150°C. Chop all the nuts and place in a large bowl.

★ Add the candied peel, apricots, pineapple, and orange rind to the nuts and mix well. Sift together the flour, unsweetened cocoa, cinnamon, coriander, nutmeg, and cloves into the bowl and mix well.

★ Put the sugar and honey into a saucepan and set over low heat, stirring, until the sugar has dissolved. Bring to a boil and cook for 5 minutes, until thickened and beginning to darken. Stir the nut mixture into the saucepan and remove from the heat.

★ Spoon the mixture into the prepared cake pan and level the surface with the back of a damp spoon. Bake in the oven for 1 hour, then transfer to a cooling rack to cool in the pan.

★ Carefully remove the cake from the pan and peel off the parchment paper. Just before serving, dredge the top with confectioners' sugar. Cut into thin wedges to serve.

Marzipan-Stuffed *Dates*

SERVES 6-8

1 lb 2 oz/500 g fresh dates
9½ oz/275 g marzipan

★ Using a small, sharp knife, cut lengthwise along the side of each date and carefully remove and discard the pit. Divide the marzipan into the same number of pieces as there are dates and roll each piece into a long oval. Insert a marzipan oval into each date and press the sides of the dates lightly together.

★ Place the stuffed dates in petit-four cases and store in an airtight container in the refrigerator until about 30 minutes before they are required. Bring to room temperature before serving.

COOK'S NOTE

★ For more elaborate petits fours, cut open and pit the dates as described in the method. Wrap a blanched almond in a small piece of marzipan, then shape into a roll with your fingers and insert into each date.

Festive

Baking

Christmas

MAKES ONE 8-INCH/20-CM CAKE

scant 1 cup raisins
¾ cup pitted dried dates, chopped
¾ cup golden raisins
3½ oz/100 g candied cherries,
    rinsed
⅔ cup brandy
1 cup butter, plus extra
    for greasing
1 cup superfine sugar
4 eggs
grated rind of 1 orange
grated rind of 1 lemon
1 tbsp blackstrap molasses
scant 1¾ cups all-purpose flour
½ tsp salt
½ tsp baking powder
1 tsp pumpkin pie spice
scant ¼ cup toasted almonds,
    chopped
scant ¼ cup toasted hazelnuts,
    chopped
1 lb 10 oz/750 g marzipan
3 tbsp apricot preserve, warmed
3 egg whites
1½ lb/650 g confectioners' sugar
silver dragées and ribbon,
    for decorating

★ Make this cake at least 3 weeks in advance. Put all the fruit in a bowl and pour over the brandy. Cover and let soak overnight.

★ Preheat the oven to 225°F/110°C. Grease an 8-inch/20-cm cake pan with butter and line it with wax paper. Cream the remaining butter and the sugar in a bowl until fluffy. Gradually beat in the eggs. Stir in the citrus rind and molasses. Sift the flour, salt, baking powder, and pumpkin pie spice into a separate bowl, then fold into the egg mixture. Fold in the soaked fruit and brandy and the nuts, then spoon the batter into the cake pan.

★ Bake in the preheated oven for at least 3 hours. If it browns too quickly, cover with foil. The cake is cooked when a skewer inserted into the center comes out clean. Remove from the oven and let cool on a cooling rack. Store in an airtight container until required.

★ Roll out the marzipan and cut to shape to cover the top and sides of the cake. Brush the cake with the preserve and press the marzipan on to the surface. Make the frosting by placing the egg whites in a bowl and adding the confectioners' sugar a little at a time, beating well until the frosting is very thick and will stand up in peaks. Spread over the covered cake, using a fork to give texture. Decorate as you wish with silver dragées and ribbon.

COOK'S NOTE

★ While the cake is being stored prior to frosting, you can pierce several holes in the top with a skewer and drizzle lightly with brandy, sherry, Madeira wine, or maraschino liqueur once a week to add extra flavor and keep it moist.

Dark Chocolate

Yule Log

SERVES 8

butter, for greasing
scant 1 cup self-rising flour,
   plus extra for dusting
³/₄ cup superfine sugar, plus extra
   for sprinkling
4 eggs, separated
1 tsp almond extract
10 oz/280 g semisweet chocolate,
   broken into squares
1 cup heavy cream
2 tbsp rum
holly, for decorating
confectioners' sugar, for dusting

⭐ Preheat the oven to 375°F/190°C. Grease with butter and line a 16 x 11-inch/ 40 x 28-cm jelly roll pan, then dust with flour.

⭐ Set aside 2 tablespoons of the superfine sugar and whisk the remainder with the egg yolks in a bowl until thick and pale. Stir in the almond extract. Whisk the egg whites in a separate grease-free bowl until soft peaks form. Gradually whisk in the reserved sugar until stiff and glossy. Sift half the flour over the egg yolk mixture and fold in, then fold in one-quarter of the egg whites. Sift and fold in the remaining flour, followed by the remaining egg whites. Spoon the batter into the pan, spreading it out evenly with a palette knife. Bake in the preheated oven for 15 minutes, until lightly golden.

⭐ Sprinkle superfine sugar over a sheet of wax paper and turn out the cake onto the paper. Roll up and let cool.

⭐ Place the chocolate in a heatproof bowl. Bring the cream to boiling point in a small saucepan, then pour it over the chocolate and stir until the chocolate has melted. Beat with an electric mixer until smooth and thick. Set aside about one-third of the chocolate mixture and stir the rum into the remainder. Unroll the cake and spread the chocolate and rum mixture over. Reroll and place on a plate or silver board. Spread the reserved chocolate mixture evenly over the top and sides. Mark with a fork so that the surface resembles tree bark. Just before serving, decorate with holly and a sprinkling of confectioners' sugar to resemble snow.

Christmas Spiced
Loaf

SERVES 6

1 lb/450 g white bread flour,
   plus extra for dusting
pinch of salt
2 tsp pumpkin pie spice
8 tbsp unsalted butter,
   chilled and diced
$^1/_6$-oz/7-g envelope active
   dry yeast
$^1/_2$ cup superfine sugar
$^3/_4$ cup currants
scant $^3/_4$ cup raisins
$^1/_4$ cup candied peel, chopped
finely grated rind of 1 orange
1 egg, beaten
$^2/_3$ cup milk, warmed
vegetable oil, for oiling

⭐ Sift the flour, salt, and pumpkin pie spice into a bowl and rub in the butter until the mixture resembles breadcrumbs. Stir in the yeast, sugar, dried fruit, candied peel, and orange rind, then add the egg and the warm milk and bring together to form a soft dough. Knead the dough briefly on a floured counter. Flour a clean bowl and add the dough. Cover the bowl and let rise in a warm place for 2 hours.

⭐ Preheat the oven to 350°F/180°C and oil a 2-lb/900-g loaf pan. Knead the dough again briefly and place it in the loaf pan, then cover and let rise for 20 minutes. Bake in the preheated oven for 1 hour 10 minutes—the loaf should be golden and well risen. Let cool in the pan.

COOK'S NOTE

⭐ To make this loaf more luxurious, you can add 3½ oz/100 g chopped marzipan to the mix before baking. Use a little egg wash to brush the loaf, and sprinkle with a little superfine sugar and ground cinnamon before baking.

Sweet Pumpkin *Pie*

SERVES 8

FILLING
4 lb/1.8 kg sweet pumpkin
1¾ cups sweetened condensed
    milk
2 eggs
½ tsp ground cinnamon
½ tsp ground nutmeg
½ tsp ground cloves
½ tsp salt
½ tsp vanilla extract
1 tbsp raw brown sugar

PIE DOUGH
4 tbsp unsalted butter,
    chilled and diced, plus extra
    for greasing
1 cup all-purpose flour, plus extra
    for dusting
¼ tsp baking powder
½ tsp ground cinnamon
¼ tsp ground nutmeg
¼ tsp ground cloves
½ tsp salt
¼ cup superfine sugar
1 egg

STREUSEL TOPPING
2 tbsp all-purpose flour
4 tbsp raw brown sugar
1 tsp ground cinnamon
2 tbsp unsalted butter,
    chilled and diced
½ cup pecans, chopped
¾ cup walnuts, chopped

★ Preheat the oven to 375°F/190°C. Halve the pumpkin, then remove and discard the seeds, stem, and stringy insides. Put the pumpkin halves, face down, in a shallow baking pan and cover with foil. Bake in the preheated oven for 1½ hours, then let cool. Scoop out the flesh and mash with a potato masher or purée in a food processor. Drain away any excess liquid. Cover with plastic wrap and chill until ready to use.

★ To make the pie dough, grease a 9-inch/23-cm round pie dish with butter. Sift the flour and baking powder into a large bowl. Stir in the spices, salt, and superfine sugar. Rub in the remaining butter until the mixture resembles fine breadcrumbs, then make a well in the center. Lightly beat the egg and pour it into the well. Mix together with a wooden spoon, then use your hands to shape the dough into a ball. Roll out on a lightly floured counter to a large round and use it to line the dish, then trim the edge. Cover with plastic wrap and chill in the refrigerator for 30 minutes.

★ Preheat the oven to 425°F/220°C. To make the filling, put the pumpkin purée in a large bowl, then stir in the condensed milk and the eggs. Add the spices and salt, then stir in the vanilla extract and raw brown sugar. Pour into the pastry shell and bake for 15 minutes.

★ Meanwhile, make the topping. Combine the flour, sugar, and cinnamon in a bowl and rub in the butter until crumbly, then stir in the nuts. Remove the pie from the oven and reduce the oven temperature to 350°F/180°C. Sprinkle the topping over the pie, then bake for an additional 35 minutes. Serve hot or cold.

Traditional

Apple Pie

SERVES 8

PIE DOUGH
2½ cups all-purpose flour
pinch of salt
6 tbsp butter or margarine,
   chilled and diced
6 tbsp lard or vegetable
   shortening, chilled and diced
about 6 tbsp cold water
beaten egg or milk, for glazing

FILLING
1 lb 10 oz–2 lb 4 oz/750 g–1 kg
   baking apples, peeled, cored,
   and sliced
scant ¾ cup light brown
   sugar or superfine sugar, plus
   extra for sprinkling
½–1 tsp ground cinnamon, pumpkin
   pie spice, or ground ginger
1–2 tbsp water (optional)

★ To make the pie dough, sift the flour and salt into a bowl. Add the butter and fat and rub in with the fingertips until the mixture resembles fine breadcrumbs. Add the water and gather the mixture together into a dough. Wrap the dough in plastic wrap and chill in the refrigerator for 30 minutes.

★ Preheat the oven to 425°F/220°C. Roll out almost two-thirds of the pie dough thinly and use to line a deep 9-inch/23-cm pie plate or pie pan.

★ To make the filling, mix the apples with the sugar and spice and pack into the pastry shell; the filling can come up above the rim. Add the water if needed, particularly if the apples are not very juicy.

★ Roll out the remaining dough to form a lid. Dampen the edges of the pie rim with water and position the lid, pressing the edges firmly together. Trim and crimp the edges. Use the trimmings to cut out leaves or other shapes to decorate the top of the pie, then dampen with water and attach. Glaze the top of the pie with beaten egg or milk and make 1–2 slits in the top, then place the pie on a baking sheet.

★ Bake in the preheated oven for 20 minutes, then reduce the oven temperature to 350°F/180°C and bake for an additional 30 minutes, until the pie dough is a light golden brown. Serve hot or cold, sprinkled with sugar.

COOK'S NOTE
★ The apples can be flavored with other spices or grated citrus rind.

Cranberry
Muffins

MAKES 18

butter, for greasing
scant 1¾ cups all-purpose flour
2 tsp baking powder
½ tsp salt
¼ cup superfine sugar
4 tbsp unsalted butter, melted
2 eggs, lightly beaten
¾ cup milk
1¼ cups fresh cranberries
1¾ oz/50 g Parmesan cheese,
    freshly grated

★ Preheat the oven to 400°F/200°C. Lightly grease two 9-cup muffin pans with butter.

★ Sift the flour, baking powder, and salt into a bowl. Stir in the sugar. Combine the butter, eggs, and milk in a separate bowl, then pour into the bowl of dry ingredients. Stir until all of the ingredients are evenly combined, then stir in the fresh cranberries.

★ Divide the batter evenly among the prepared 18 cups in the muffin pans. Sprinkle the grated Parmesan cheese over the top. Bake in the preheated oven for 20 minutes, until risen and golden.

★ Remove the muffins from the oven and let cool slightly in the pans. Put the muffins on a cooling rack and let cool completely.

COOK'S NOTE

★ For a sweeter alternative, replace the Parmesan cheese with raw brown sugar.

Gingerbread *House*

MAKES 1 HOUSE

9 tbsp unsalted butter,
    chilled and diced, plus extra
    for greasing
scant 3 cups self-rising flour
scant ³/₄ cup light brown sugar
1½ tsp ground ginger
½ tsp ground cloves
1 tsp ground cinnamon
⅓ cup blackstrap molasses
1 large egg, beaten
1 lb 2 oz/500 g easy-spread white
    royal frosting
soft frosting, for piping
candies, cookies, and dragées,
    for decorating

✦ Grease 2 baking sheets with butter and line with parchment paper. Sift the flour into a large bowl and rub in the remaining butter until the mixture resembles breadcrumbs. Stir in the sugar and spices. In a separate bowl, whisk the molasses with the egg and pour onto the dry ingredients. Stir to combine and mix to a smooth dough. Wrap in plastic wrap and chill for 30 minutes.

✦ Preheat the oven to 400°F/200°C. Divide the dough into 6 pieces and keep the unrolled dough wrapped in plastic wrap. You will need to roll the dough out to ¼ inch/5 mm thick and cut 6 pieces for the house—the easiest method is to use cardboard or paper templates. Cut 2 pieces for the side walls (6¼ x 4 inches/16 x 10 cm), 2 for the end walls (4½ inches/12 cm wide and 6½ inches/17 cm at the tip of the "gable"), and 2 for the roof (7 x 4½ inches/ 18 x 12 cm). Cut out a window in one of the side walls and a door in the front.

✦ Lay the pieces of dough on the baking sheets and bake in the oven for 10 to 12 minutes, until slightly risen and evenly cooked. Let cool slightly on the baking sheets, then transfer to a cooling rack to cool completely.

✦ To assemble the house, spread a line of royal frosting on a cake board and position a "wall" on it. Using small glasses to support it, spread a little more frosting on the ends and board and attach the other "walls." Let the house set for 30 minutes and make sure that it is standing securely before adding more frosting to attach the roof pieces. Let set before spreading on more frosting over the roof, pulling the frosting over the edge to create "icicles." Use soft frosting to pipe along the joins. Decorate with candies, cookies, and dragées.

Shortbread
Slices

MAKES 16

COOKIE BASE
9 tbsp salted butter,
 plus extra for greasing
¼ cup superfine sugar
1¼ cups all-purpose flour

TOPPING
½ cup superfine sugar
8 tbsp salted butter
scant 1 cup condensed milk
2 tbsp dark corn syrup
7 oz/200 g mixed dried fruit
scant ¾ cup mixed chopped nuts
7 oz/200 g milk chocolate,
 broken into pieces

★ Preheat the oven to 325°F/160°C. Grease a 9-inch/23-cm square cake pan with butter and line it with wax paper.

★ Dice the remaining butter, then place in a bowl with the sugar and flour and rub together to form a crumbly dough. Press firmly and evenly into the prepared cake pan and bake in the preheated oven for 30 to 35 minutes, until golden. Let cool in the pan.

★ To make the toffee for the topping, melt the sugar and 7 tablespoons of the butter together slowly in a pan, then let simmer for 10 minutes until thick. Add the condensed milk and syrup and bring gently to a boil, stirring continuously. Reduce the heat and cook the toffee, scraping down the sides of the pan, for 5 to 10 minutes, until the mixture is golden and thick—be careful not to overcook it. Pour over the cookie base. Scatter over the fruit and nuts and press gently into the toffee. Let set in the refrigerator for 20 minutes.

★ Meanwhile, put the chocolate and the remaining butter in a heatproof bowl, then set over a saucepan of barely simmering water and heat until melted and smooth. Spread the chocolate mixture over the set toffee and chill in the refrigerator for 2 hours. Cut the shortbread into 16 squares with a hot knife.

COOK'S NOTE

★ Instead of adding the fruit and nut layer, you can decorate the top with chopped candied cherries or chopped nuts, drizzled white chocolate or chocolate-covered nuts.

Cheesecake with *Pecans*

SERVES 6-8

BASE
⅓ cup pecans
5½ oz/150 g graham crackers, broken into pieces
3½ tbsp salted butter, melted

FILLING
1¾ cups cream cheese
scant 1 cup curd cheese
scant ¾ cup superfine sugar
3 large eggs
3 large egg yolks
scant 1 cup heavy cream

TOPPING
butter, for greasing
heaping 1 cup superfine sugar
5 tbsp water
scant ½ cup pecans

★ Preheat the oven to 325°F/160°C. To make the base, put the pecans in a food processor and process briefly, then add the broken crackers and pulse again to form crumbs. Tip into a bowl and stir in the melted butter until well combined. Press this into the base of an 8-inch/20-cm springform cake pan. Bake in the preheated oven for 10 minutes. Let cool.

★ To make the filling, beat the cream cheese, curd cheese, and sugar together in a large bowl. Beat in the eggs and egg yolks, one at a time, until smooth. Finally, stir in the cream. Spoon over the prepared base. Bake in the preheated oven for 1 hour, then test—the cheesecake should be cooked but with a slight "wobble" in the center. Return to the oven for an additional 10 minutes if necessary. Let cool in the pan.

★ To make the topping, grease a piece of foil with butter and lay it flat. Put the sugar and water in a saucepan and heat gently, stirring, until the sugar has dissolved. Bring to a simmer, swirling the saucepan rather than stirring, and cook until the syrup begins to darken to form the caramel, then add the pecans. Lift each pecan out onto the greased foil and let harden. When you are ready to serve, unmold the cheesecake onto a serving plate and arrange the caramel pecans on top.

COOK'S NOTE

★ This cheesecake can be topped with any number of ingredients instead of the pecans—try cranberries cooked with orange rind and sugar, cooled, and then spooned on top, or simply top with the seeds and juice of 6 passion fruit before serving.

Christmas Frosted

Ginger Cake

SERVES 6-8

¾ cup unsalted butter, softened
scant 1 cup superfine sugar
3 large eggs, beaten
1 tbsp blackstrap molasses
2 tbsp ginger syrup
scant 1¾ cups self-rising flour
1 tsp ground ginger
1 tsp ground allspice
1 tbsp ground almonds
2 tbsp whole milk
2½ oz/70 g preserved ginger,
   chopped
edible gold leaf or silver leaf,
   for decorating

FROSTING
2¼ cups confectioners' sugar
1 tsp ginger syrup

⭐ Preheat the oven to 325°F/160°C. Grease a 6 x 10-inch/15 x 25-cm square cake pan and line with wax paper.

⭐ Cream the butter and superfine sugar in a large bowl until pale and fluffy. Put the eggs and molasses into a pitcher with the ginger syrup and whisk together. Sift the flour and spices onto a plate. Alternately add a little of the egg mixture and then a spoonful of the flour mixture to the butter and sugar mixture until you have used up both. Add the almonds and milk and mix together until you have a smooth mixture. Fold in the preserved ginger pieces.

⭐ Spoon the cake batter into the prepared pan and level the surface with a palette knife, then bake in the preheated oven for 45 to 50 minutes, until well risen and firm to the touch. Let cool in the pan for 10 minutes, then turn out onto a cooling rack to cool completely.

⭐ To make the frosting, put the confectioners' sugar in a large bowl. Beat in the ginger syrup and just enough cold water to make a thick frosting—be careful not to add too much water too quickly. Remove the cake from the pan and spread the frosting over the top, letting it run down the sides. Decorate with edible gold or silver leaf.

COOK'S NOTE

⭐ For a slightly different effect, you could decorate with extra chopped preserved ginger.

Christmas Tree
Cookies

MAKES 12

heaping 1 cup all-purpose flour,
    plus extra for dusting
1 tsp ground cinnamon
½ tsp ground nutmeg
½ tsp ground ginger
5 tbsp unsalted butter, diced, plus
    extra for greasing
3 tbsp honey

FOR DECORATING
white frosting (optional)
narrow gold or silver ribbon

★ Sift the flour and spices into a bowl and rub in the butter until the mixture resembles breadcrumbs. Add the honey and mix together well to form a soft dough. Wrap the dough in plastic wrap and chill in the refrigerator for 30 minutes.

★ Meanwhile, preheat the oven to 350°F/180°C and lightly grease 2 baking sheets with butter. Divide the dough in half. Roll out 1 piece of dough on a floured counter to about ¼ inch/5 mm thick. Cut out tree shapes using a cutter or cardboard template. Repeat with the remaining piece of dough.

★ Put the cookies on the prepared baking sheets and, using a toothpick, make a hole through the top of each cookie large enough to thread the ribbon through. Chill in the refrigerator for 15 minutes.

★ Bake the cookies in the preheated oven for 10 to 12 minutes, until golden. Let cool on the baking sheets for 5 minutes, then transfer to a cooling rack to cool completely. Decorate the trees with white frosting, or simply leave them plain, then thread a length of ribbon through each hole and knot. Hang from the Christmas tree.

COOK'S NOTE

★ Frost these cookies with a mixture of colored frosting and silver dragées, and hang on the tree with matching ribbon, or put into cellophane bags and tie with a matching ribbon to give to friends.

Brown Sugar &
Cinnamon Rolls

MAKES 12

1 lb/450 g all-purpose flour, plus
    extra for dusting
1½ tsp salt
1 tbsp superfine sugar
2 tsp active dry yeast
1 cup tepid whole milk
vegetable oil, for oiling
scant ½ cup light brown sugar
1½ tsp ground cinnamon
1 egg, beaten

★ Mix the flour, salt, superfine sugar, and yeast together in a large bowl. Stir in the milk to form a dough. Knead the dough on a floured counter until smooth and pliable. Put in a clean bowl, then cover the bowl and let rise in a warm place for 2 hours.

★ Meanwhile, preheat the oven to 400°F/200°C and oil 2 baking sheets. Knock back the dough and knead briefly again on a floured counter, then roll out to a rectangle measuring 12 x 9½ inches/30 x 24 cm. Mix ¼ cup of the light brown sugar with the cinnamon and sprinkle over the surface. Press into the dough, then roll up the dough tightly like a jelly roll and cut into 12 evenly sized pieces. Lay each piece on its side on the prepared baking sheets and cover with a clean dish towel, then let rise in a warm place for 30 minutes.

★ Brush the rolls with the egg and sprinkle over the remaining light brown sugar. Bake in the preheated oven for 12 to 15 minutes, until golden—be careful not to overcook and burn them. Transfer to a cooling rack to cool.

COOK'S NOTE

★ For an easy vacation breakfast, you can make this dough ahead of time and freeze it—simply thaw and brush with the egg and sugar before baking.

Craft
Proje

*M*aking your own cards and decorations is definitely worth the effort, if you have the time, because everyone appreciates all those personal finishing touches. In the following pages, there are 16 projects for you to try, from simple Christmas Snowflake Cards and elegant Festive Napkin Holders to the luxurious Truffle Tree and stunning Star Tree Topper. There is something for every aspect of Christmas, and the projects are relatively easy to make, so the whole family can get involved.

cts

Making your own
Craft Projects

Add a personal touch to Christmas by making your own festive cards, gift tags, tree decorations, garlands, and even elegant centerpieces for the dinner table. The following projects are all quite easy to make and do not need any specialist equipment or materials.

*I*mpress your family and friends this Christmas by handcrafting one or several of the following unique cards and decorations. All these items make memorable gifts, but they can also be used to bring an individual, imaginative dimension to your own festive display. Instead of expending energy and effort on frantic shopping expeditions, let these inspirational ideas fire your creative flair within the comfort of your own home. A gift made by hand, especially tailored to the recipient with thought, care, and love, is simply priceless!

THE PROJECTS
The following pages present 16 projects, ranging from simple gift tags and cards that cleverly incorporate a detachable tree decoration in their

design, which are relatively easy-and-quick to make, to those that require a little more time and effort, such as the traditional Christmas Door Wreath, the Country-Style Garland, and the luxurious Truffle Tree, which could form the focus of your Christmas entertaining. There are also other inventive ideas for the seasonal table, such as beaded napkin holders and a bejeweled wire centerpiece, while the elegant Reindeer Tealight Box will add a warming glow to any room. Otherwise, consider making a gift of a festively framed family photo, which will be treasured for years to come, or create a fun fabric advent calendar. All these projects can be achieved with ease by even the novice crafter, involving only basic papercrafting, sewing, and other handicraft skills. The clear and concise directions in each project will guide you reassuringly step by step through each stage of the construction.

EQUIPMENT AND MATERIALS

The projects require only basic household tools and materials, and those who enjoy crafts are likely to have many of the items already. In fact, no power equipment is involved, except a steam iron! Even the sewing is done by hand, but you can use a sewing machine if you prefer. A list of exactly what is needed is given for each project.

TEMPLATES

Templates are given where appropriate (see pages 218–221), and can be simply enlarged on a photocopier as directed, or sized according to your own requirements.

SAFETY PRECAUTIONS

- Work in well-lit conditions, to avoid accidents or damaging your eyesight.
- Wear protective clothing (face mask and gloves) when using toxic substances, such as spray paints and glues.
- Keep sharp tools, adhesives, or any other potentially harmful items or substances safely out of the reach of babies and young children.

Whenever you use an art knife, be sure to:
- Use a cutting mat.
- Use a steel rule and cut against the steel edge.
- Change the blade regularly and discard old blades responsibly.

Embroidery Stitches

- Simple embroidery stitches are used in some of the projects. The following diagrams show how to do a cross-stitch and a blanket stitch.

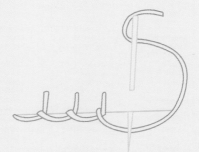

cross-stitch

blanket stitch

Christmas Card
Tree Decoration

Would you like to give something a little more than a card, but you are not sure of what to buy? This clever card design doubles up as a stylish tree decoration.

MATERIALS

* 300 gsm brown card
* pale-green plain paper
* pale-green handmade-quality paper
* brown, red, and gold glitter card
* brown corrugated card
* 3¼-inch/8-cm length of ¼-inch/5-mm wide dark-red ribbon
* 4½-inch/12-cm length of 1⁄16-inch/2-mm wide green ribbon
* deep-red glass bead, about ½–⅝ inch/10-15 mm in diameter
* small, double-backed self-adhesive pad
* pencil, art knife, steel rule, cutting mat, bone folder or scoring tool, hole punch, glue stick, double-sided tape

★ Enlarge the template on page 220 on a photocopier to the required size and cut out. Draw around the template onto the brown card and cut out with an art knife and steel rule on a cutting mat. Score down the center with a bone folder or scoring tool and fold. Punch a hole near the top.

★ Cover the inside of the tree with glue stick. Stick the plain green paper on one half of the inside, placing it down the center fold and making sure it adheres well. Trim with the art knife. Repeat on the opposite side. Cut out the punched hole with the art knife.

★ Cut a trunk from brown glitter card and attach in two pieces to the front and back of the card with double-sided tape. Cut the container from brown corrugated card and attach in the same way.

★ Attach the red ribbon with double-sided tape, running it over the card spine.

★ Use glue stick to adhere the green handmade-quality paper in one piece to the front and back of the outside of the card. Cut out the punched hole.

★ Create a loop for hanging from the green ribbon, threading the deep-red glass bead onto it before tying off. Attach the self-adhesive pad to the inside of the card for the recipient to use to fasten the card closed.

Angel Card

Tree Decoration

This delightful card design incorporates a balsa wood angel that can be lifted from the card to hang on the Christmas tree.

MATERIALS

* 300 gsm white card
* gold paper
* small-weave hessian
* scrap card
* large-weave hessian
* scrap of board 1/16 inch/ 2 mm thick
* balsa wood 1/8 inch/ 3 mm thick
* acrylic paints: white, cadmium yellow
* gold enamel paint
* thin craft wire
* pencil, art knife, steel rule, cutting mat, bone folder or scoring tool, double-sided tape, black felt-tip pen, paintbrush, long-nosed pliers, pin, superglue

✹ Using an art knife and steel rule on a cutting mat, cut a piece of the white card 6⅛ x 7½ inches/15.5 x 19 cm. Score down the center with a bone folder or a scoring tool and fold in half. Attach the gold paper to the front of the folded card with double-sided tape. Trim with the art knife and steel rule. Cut a piece of small-weave hessian 6⅛ x 3¾ inches/15.5 x 9.5 cm. Use an existing frayed edge for the right-hand edge or fray by pulling a few vertical strands away. Attach the hessian with double-sided tape so that it fits exactly over the gold paper.

✹ Enlarge the templates on page 218 on a photocopier as directed and cut out. Draw around the templates onto scrap card and cut out with an art knife and steel rule on a cutting mat.

✹ Draw around the angel silhouette onto the large-weave hessian with the black felt-tip pen and cut out. Attach to the card with double-sided tape.

✹ Using the template, cut a large heart from gold paper and attach it to a piece of board with double-sided tape, then attach to the hessian angel. Open the card and lay flat, then cut a small upside-down "V" in the top edge of the card front. This will serve as a hook for the balsa wood angel.

✹ Using the templates and art knife, cut the wings, angel body, and small heart from balsa wood. Paint the head and wings with white acrylic paint. Add a tiny amount of cadmium yellow to the white to make a cream for the dress. While drying, paint the heart with gold enamel paint. Cut a 5-inch/13-cm length of wire with the pliers and twist the ends together for a length of ½ inch/1 cm, forming a hoop for the halo.

✹ Paint white polka dots on the dress. When dry, superglue the angel body to the wings, and the heart to the body. Using the pin, make a hole at the top of the wings behind the angel's back. Superglue the twisted wire of the halo into the hole.

Christmas

Snowflake Cards

Just one template can be used to create four classy card designs that will look stunning on display in the home. You can, of course, use different colored papers and spray paints to create a color scheme of your choice.

MATERIALS

* card ⅛ inch/3 mm thick
* 300 gsm Bockingford (slightly textured) paper
* 300 gsm white card
* silver and/or gold spray paint
* silver and/or gold card
* pencil, art knife, steel rule, cutting mat, painter's tape, bone folder or scoring tool, double-sided tape, old newspaper, face mask, and protective gloves

★ Enlarge the template on page 220 on a photocopier as directed and cut out with scissors. Draw around the template onto the ⅛-inch/3-mm thick card and cut out with an art knife and steel rule on a cutting mat.

★ Place the template on the Bockingford paper and secure with painter's tape. Ensure there is enough space to create a 6-inch/ 15-cm square. Turn the paper over and rub firmly all over the template area with a bone folder to create an impression.

★ Remove the template. Ensure that the embossed snowflake is in the center of the paper, then trim to 6 inches/15 cm square.

★ Cut a piece of white card 6 x 12 inches/ 15 x 30 cm. Score down the center with a bone folder and fold in half. Use double-sided tape around the edges of the embossed snowflake panel to attach it to the card.

★ Repeat steps 2 to 4 to create a second card, but adhere the Bockingford paper to the opposite side of the white card to create a reversed impression.

★ To make a third card, place the template on the front of folded white card (see step 4). Protect your counter with old newspaper. Wearing a face mask and protective gloves, spray silver and/or gold paint over the card. When dry, remove the template to reveal the snowflake.

★ To make a fourth card, cut a piece of silver or gold card 6 x 12 inches/15 x 30 cm. Score down the center with a bone folder or scoring tool and fold in half. Respray the snowflake template so that it contrasts with the card, if needed, and attach it to the card front with double-sided tape.

Christmas Card
Snowmen

Bring a smile to someone's face with this fun, quirky snowman card, with its three-dimensional quality. The arms of the metal foil snowmen are flexible enough to bring gently forward to create more shadow behind.

MATERIALS

* 300 gsm white card
* scrap card
* roll of pewter lightweight metal foil
* 90 gsm white paper
* thick tracing paper 4³⁄₈ inches/11.5 cm square
* 2 ready-made embossed snowflakes, about 1³⁄₄ inches/4.5 cm in diameter
* pencil, art knife, steel rule, cutting mat, bone folder or scoring tool, permanent black marker pen, wool needle, hole punch, double-sided tape, superglue

Using an art knife and a steel rule on a cutting mat, cut a piece of the white card 4³⁄₄ x 10 inches/12.5 x 25 cm. Score down the center with a bone folder or a scoring tool and fold in half. Copy the template on page 221 on a photocopier and cut out. Draw around the template onto scrap card and cut out with an art knife and steel rule on a cutting mat. Draw around the template three times onto the foil using the marker pen.

Cut the snowmen out with the art knife, but slightly change each one to give them individual character. For example, make the first snowman's hat taller, the second one's body larger, and the third one's face a different shape.

Cut a strip of pewter foil ³⁄₈ x 4³⁄₈ inches/7 mm x 11.5 cm. Dab it all over with the wool needle to create texture. Punch about 24 dots from the white paper.

Attach the pewter strip about ¹⁄₄ inch/7 mm from the bottom of the tracing paper with double-sided tape. Place double-sided tape on the reverse of the tracing paper and pewter strip, and attach to the folded card, positioning it centrally.

Carefully lift the tracing paper to attach the embossed snowflakes to the card with double-sided tape. Add a few paper dots, ensuring that there are two in either top corner. Place a droplet of superglue on each of these corner dots to fasten the tracing paper securely. Stick another two paper dots to the tracing paper to hide the glue marks.

Attach the snowmen at different angles with double-sided tape, ensuring that they are butted up against the pewter strip. Add the remaining paper dots around the snowmen.

Tree Table *Decoration*

Bring a touch of elegance to your festive table with this unusual tree centerpiece. It can be made bigger or smaller by varying the number of hoops.

MATERIALS

* craft wire—thick (1/16 inch/2 mm) and thin
* 6 cylindrical objects descending in diameter, such as: plant pot measuring 5 inches/13 cm in diameter, body of wine bottle, mug, body lotion bottle, correction fluid bottle, neck of wine bottle
* reel of silver thread
* 39-inch/1-meter strings of silver beads in 3 varieties
* tiny glass turquoise and cobalt blue beads
* blue sequins
* 3 cobalt-blue glass droplets
* 3 cobalt-blue plastic leaf beads
* 4 turquoise glass "bunches of grapes" beads
* silver elastic
* blue and clear plastic gems
* clear glass star with a hole, 1 inch/2.5 cm in diameter
* tack lifter, tape measure, superglue

★ To make 6 wire hoops, wrap a length of the thick wire around each cylindrical object in turn. Leave some surplus, then cut with the tack lifter. Twist the ends together to make each hoop fit tightly around the object, then trim the twisted wire to remove any protruding ends

★ To create the "trunk", cut a length of thick wire equal to the total of the height of the tree, half the diameter of the base hoop and an extra 3/4 inch/2 cm to allow enough wire to attach it to the base hoop. So, for a tree 12 inches/30 cm high and with 5-inch/13-cm base hoop, you would need a 15 1/4-inch/38.5-cm length of wire. Use the first 1/4–1/2 inch/5–10 mm of the wire to form a loop. With the wire upright above the center of the base hoop, make a right-angled bend 12 inches/30 cm from the top loop. Twist the last 5/8 inch/1.5 cm around the base hoop with the tack lifter.

★ Cut a piece of the thin wire equal in length to the diameter of the next-largest hoop, plus 1 1/2 inches/4 cm to attach the hoop to the "trunk." At the halfway point along the wire, wrap it around the trunk 2 inches/5 cm from the base hoop. Twist either end around opposite points on the hoop. Cut 4 pieces of the wire 3 1/4 inches/8 cm long. With each length, twist 5/8 inch/1.5 cm at either end around the base hoop and the one above it at evenly spaced intervals. Attach the remaining hoops in the same way. Use 3 pieces of wire 2 inches/5 cm long to attach the smallest hoop to the small top loop.

★ Secure the end of the silver thread to the base hoop with superglue, then weave it all over the tree and glue to the top of the tree. Repeat with the strings of silver beads. Thread blue beads and sequins onto the thin wire and twist around the tree, securing either end by twisting around the hoops. Hang the glass droplets and other decorative beads at intervals from little loops of wire. Thread some onto silver elastic, using knots to secure them in place at various points. Superglue the blue and clear plastic gems in place. Use the wire to attach the glass star to the tree top.

TIP

★ Ensure there are no potentially harmful wire ends protruding by bending them toward the trunk with the tack lifter.

Festive *Mobile*

Welcome family and friends into your home in style this Christmas by hanging this richly colored mobile in your hallway.

MATERIALS

- ★ light-green, dark-green, cream, and dark-red felt
- ★ large sewing needle and embroidery thread: dark-red, sage-green, and cream
- ★ wadding
- ★ 4 fabric hearts, about ⁵⁄₈ inch/1.5 cm wide
- ★ 4 red or wooden buttons, about ³⁄₄ inch/2 cm in diameter
- ★ brass bell, about ³⁄₄ inch/ 2 cm in diameter
- ★ red and dark-green ribbon
- ★ inner wooden ring of an embroidery hoop, 8 inches/ 20 cm in diameter
- ★ natural string
- ★ 8 red beads, about ¹⁄₄ inch/ 5 mm in diameter
- ★ reel of transparent elastic
- ★ craft wire
- ★ scissors, tailor's chalk, art knife, cutting mat, fabric glue, double-sided tape, superglue, tack lifter, clear nail polish

★ Enlarge the templates on page 220 on a photocopier as directed and cut out with scissors. Use tailor's chalk and either scissors or an art knife and a cutting mat to cut 2 of the following from felt: light-green bell; dark-green star; cream rocking horse, and heart; red soldier.

★ Using the pattern on page 220, cross-stitch a heart in both cream hearts. Hand sew the hearts and the other pairs of shapes together with a blanket stitch (see page 185)—use dark-red thread for the cream shapes and the bell, cream for the star, and sage-green for the soldier. Just before you finish stitching each shape, slightly stuff with wadding. Using fabric glue, stick the fabric hearts to the rocking horse and star on either side.

★ Cover one side of 2 buttons with red felt and 2 with green felt using double-sided tape. Using sage green thread, sew through each button once, then tie a knot at the back and trim the thread. Using fabric glue, stick a red button on either side of the bell and a green button on either side of the soldier. Sew the brass bell to the felt bell.

★ Tightly wrap red and green ribbon around the wooden hoop and use double-sided tape and superglue to fasten and secure it. Repeat with the string, wrapping it close together in some parts and spaced out in others to reveal the ribbon.

★ Cut different lengths of string for all the shapes except the heart, ranging from 17³⁄₄ inches/45 cm for the rocking horse to 2 inches/5 cm for the bell. Thread beads onto the strings and secure with knots at various points. Loop each string over the ring and superglue both ends to the top of each shape, positioning as shown.

★ Attach 4 evenly spaced lengths of transparent elastic to the ring, then join together onto a wire loop, formed with the tack lifter, which can be used to attach the mobile to the ceiling. Sew a 10-inch/25-cm length of elastic to the center top of the heart, then tie the other end to the metal loop and seal with clear nail polish.

Snowflake *Gift Box*

This unusually shaped gift box is as practical as it is attractive. After you have made the printed fabric, you can use the silver snowflakes to make pretty confetti for the table.

MATERIALS

* sheet of paper
* old newspaper
* white cotton fabric 20 inches/50 cm square
* silver spray paint
* scrap card
* card 1/16 inch/2 mm thick
* matte silver paper
* felt-backed paper—black, silver, cream, or light-blue
* tissue paper
* 300 gsm white card
* silver elastic
* art knife, cutting mat, face mask and protective gloves, spray glue, hair spray, steel rule, gel superglue, strong self-adhesive binding tape, strong double-sided tape

★ Enlarge the snowflake template on page 220 on a photocopier at various sizes—no set size is required, but you should be able to fit the largest snowflake onto one side of the box. Using scissors, cut around the outlines and attach to fill a sheet of paper. Photocopy the sheet 3 times. Cut out each snowflake with an art knife on a cutting mat.

★ Lay the newspaper down in a well-ventilated area, then lay the white cotton fabric on top, ensuring that it is not creased. Wearing a face mask and protective gloves, spray the snowflakes with glue and scatter onto the cotton fabric, pressing down firmly around the edges. Spray the snowflakes and cotton with silver paint. Let dry. Remove the silver snowflakes, then spray the cotton lightly with hair spray to seal.

★ Enlarge the box templates on page 221 on a photocopier as directed and cut out with scissors. Draw around the templates onto scrap card and cut out with an art knife and steel rule on a cutting mat.

★ Using the templates, cut all the pieces for the box out of the 1/16-inch/2-mm thick card. Place the base on newspaper and run gel superglue along one longer edge. Hold one of the sides vertically butted up against the base until completely dry and rigid. Repeat for the opposite side. Add the ends to the base and sides in the same way. Add the lid, using strong self-adhesive binding tape on the outside and inside, ensuring there is a gap of about 1/16 inch/ 2 mm (where the binding tape on the front and back will touch) to allow a good hinge.

★ Starting with the lid, coat each box side with double-sided tape, including the edges. Adhere to the reverse of the cotton fabric and trim with the art knife. Ensure that you leave enough fabric to wrap over the edges for a good finish. Line the inside with silver paper and the bottom with felt-backed paper. Add tissue paper.

★ Cut a gift-tag shape from the white card. Cover with offcuts of the cotton using double-sided tape, then thread with silver elastic. The elastic can be tied in a loop and stretched over the box to close it.

Gift *Tags*

A gift tag makes the perfect embellishment to a beautifully wrapped present, and here are a few ideas for making your own. These tags can also be made larger as greeting cards.

MATERIALS

HOLLY AND HEART TAGS

* 300 gsm white, green, or red card
* red and sage-green felt
* sewing needle and deep-red embroidery thread
* holly leaf
* deep-red raw-silk fabric scraps
* red ribbon

PERSONALIZED PHOTO TAG

* 300 gsm white or red card
* gold or silver acrylic paint/ink
* family photograph
* red felt-tip pen
* correction fluid
* fine black pen
* pencil, art knife, steel rule, cutting mat, hole punch, strong double-sided tape, old newspaper, paintbrush, bone folder

HOLLY AND HEART TAGS

★ Choose any color card to make your gift tag to the size you require. Cut out a rectangular shape with an art knife and steel rule on a cutting mat. Punch a hole in the corner.

★ Attach the red felt to the holly tag and the green felt to the heart tag with double-sided tape. Trim with the art knife.

★ Using the sewing needle and embroidery thread, sew the holly leaf to the felt side of the tag with one cross-stitch (see page 185), tying the thread at the back and trimming the excess.

★ Cut 3 small squares of the silk and, using double-sided tape, adhere to the felt side of the heart tag, overlapping them at jaunty angles. Add a small sage green felt heart to one of the silk squares with double-sided tape.

★ Carefully cut the punched holes in the tags with the art knife, then thread a length of red ribbon through each hole and make a knot in the ribbon.

PERSONALIZED PHOTO TAG

★ For the photo tag, enlarge the template on page 221 as directed and cut out with scissors. Transfer to the white or red card. Cut out, using an art knife and a cutting mat, including the square window in the center, but leave the white areas inside the bow (you can also cut them out).

★ Protect your counter with old newspaper. Paint the light gray areas on the template with gold or silver paint, or ink, to complete the frame.

★ Take a black-and-white photocopy of the photograph, or print out a black-and-white copy, to fit the size of the tag window. Duplicate the image as many times as required. Add Santa Claus hats with red felt-tip pen and bobbles with correction fluid. When dry, outline the hats with a fine black pen. Cut the image out, leaving a border (especially at the top) to adhere it to the frame with double-sided tape. Adhere a folded card to the back of the tag for writing a message. Attach the tag to your gift with double-sided tape.

Country-Style *Garland*

Perfect for creating a country cottage feel, this New England-style garland will bring warmth and traditional festive cheer to your home. Choose to make several short ones or a few longer ones to fit any size of wall, mantel, or stairwell.

MATERIALS

- ✷ small-weave hessian fabric 12 inches/30 cm square
- ✷ large-weave hessian fabric 12 inches/30 cm square
- ✷ scraps of pale-green and deep-red felt
- ✷ scraps of deep-red gingham and plain red cotton fabric
- ✷ natural string
- ✷ decorative gold fine thread or ribbon
- ✷ 5 red buttons, ¾ inch/2 cm in diameter
- ✷ embroidery needle and deep-red embroidery thread
- ✷ thin craft wire
- ✷ 6 tiny wooden pegs
- ✷ 2 tiny felt hearts
- ✷ scissors, tailor's chalk, art knife, cutting mat, tape measure, fabric glue, tack lifter, strong double-sided tape

✦ Enlarge the templates on page 218 on a photocopier as directed and cut out using scissors. Using tailor's chalk and either scissors or an art knife on a cutting mat, cut out the following: 2 circles from small-weave hessian, 2 from large-weave hessian; 2 large stars from each hessian, 1 small star from green felt; 4 angel bodies from large-weave hessian; 4 angel wings from small-weave hessian; 2 large hearts from red gingham, 2 from plain red; 2 small hearts from red gingham, 2 from plain red, 2 from green felt.

✦ Lay a 59-inch/1.5 m length of string on a counter and twist the gold thread around. Tie a loop at either end and fray the ends.

✦ Cover one side of the buttons with fabric glue and adhere the red felt. Cut around the buttons with an art knife. Pass the needle and thread through the buttonholes once so the thread ends dangle from the back of the button by about ⅝ inch/1.5 cm. Ensure 2 of the buttons have extra thread hanging.

✦ Arrange the embellishments above the string, working out from the center. Run a length of thin wire around the top of the red and gingham large hearts with the tack lifter and use double-sided tape to sandwich between the fabrics. Glue a small green heart to the plain red side and add one of the buttons. Use 2 pegs to attach to the string.

✦ Construct the angels in the same way, but simply sandwich the string in between the head and tops of the wings. Sandwich the wings (2 sets per angel) in between the bodies. Glue the tiny felt hearts in place.

✦ Construct the remaining embellishments in the same way, using wire to strengthen them, and attach to the string.

Christmas Door *Wreath*

This simple but effective door decoration will be admired by all who visit, yet doesn't demand any sophisticated floristry skills. For an alternative look, experiment with various fabric combinations, ribbons, and string, and use other embellishments in place of the holly, bearing in mind that it needs to withstand the weather conditions if not sheltered.

MATERIALS

* plain deep-red fabric, red gingham and ruby raw-silk fabric, each 1 inch x 59 inches/ 2.5 cm x 1.5 meters
* polystyrene wreath 9½ inches/24 cm in diameter
* red gingham 1 x 20 inches/ 2.5 cm x 50 cm
* 21 holly leaves, 16 about 2½ inches/6 cm in length and 5 about 1½ inches/4 cm in length
* floristry wire
* 2 fir cones on wire about 2 inches/5 cm in length
* fake berries on flexible stems
* tape measure, scissors, strong double-sided tape, tack lifter

★ Wrap the red fabric strip around the wreath—the point at which you start and finish will become the bottom of the wreath. Use double-sided tape to secure the ends. Do not worry about covering all the polystyrene at this stage.

★ Repeat with the larger length of gingham, starting and ending in the same place and focusing on covering more of the polystyrene. Repeat with the raw silk to cover the remaining polystyrene.

★ Wrap the smaller piece of gingham over where the other strips started and ended as many times as possible, tying the ends in a tight knot. Trim the ends. Use the scissors to trim any stray threads.

★ Thread all the holly leaves with the floristry wire, using the tack lifter to help direct the wire into the main veins of the holly. The smaller leaves should be together. Use the tack lifter to pierce all around the polystyrene wreath and insert the large holly leaves into the holes. The smaller leaves should be by the wrapped gingham.

★ Gently push the fir cones under the wrapped gingham with the berries, and finish with the smaller wired holly in between. Push a length of wire into the back of the wreath to make a loop to hang the wreath.

Festive *Frame*

Frame your family members in festive spirit. If you have the time, make one for each family member in a different size for a special collection.

MATERIALS

* image transfer paste
* color photocopy or printout of family photograph
* white cotton fabric 7 inches/18 cm square
* 300 gsm white card
* foam board, ¼ inch/5 mm thick, measuring 10¼ x 12½ inches/25.5 x 31 cm
* deep-red cotton fabric 20 inches/50 cm square
* ¼-inch/5-mm thick board 12 inches/30 cm square
* ruby-red raw-silk 6 x 12 inches/15 x 30 cm
* 8-inch/20-cm length of ¼-inch/7-mm wide ruby-red ribbon
* 12-inch/30-cm length of ⅛-inch/3-mm wide green ribbon
* 6 holly leaves, about 1½ inches/4 cm in length
* wired fake red berries
* 300 gsm deep-red card
* metal picture hook
* sponge, paintbrush, paper towels, rolling pin, art knife, steel rule, cutting mat, strong double-sided tape, superglue

★ Using the image transfer paste, transfer your image onto the white cotton. When dry, back it with the white card using double-sided tape, ensuring that the fabric is taut.

★ Cut a square of foam board large enough to frame your image. Cut an aperture in the board to give your image a ¾-inch/2-cm wide white cotton border.

★ Stick double-sided tape around the edges of the foam board frame on both sides. Adhere the red cotton fabric tightly to the frame front. Cut 2 diagonal lines joining the two sets of opposing inner corners of the frame. Fold the triangles back, pull tightly, and adhere to the frame back. Trim the excess. At each corner, make two cuts from the outer edges of the fabric to form a right angle and cut away the fabric corners. Fold the fabric neatly over the frame, pull tightly, and adhere to the frame. Trim the excess. Use scraps of fabric to cover up any exposed foam.

★ Place the thick board square on the silk fabric and cut around it with an art knife on a cutting mat. Cut as many squares as you need to cover just under half the height of the frame. Attach double-sided tape to the squares to prevent fraying. Attach to the frame, alternating the weave from horizontal to vertical, folding the fabric over the sides. At the frame corners, snip the fabric diagonally into the corner and fold over the frame.

★ Place double-sided tape onto the red ribbon and use to trim the top of the silk squares. Repeat with the green ribbon, about ½ inch/1 cm from the top. Use double-sided tape to secure the ends to the back.

★ "Hang" the holly leaves from the green ribbon with double-sided tape, three either side of the wired fake berries, which are hooked over the top edge of the frame.

★ Place double-sided tape on the four corners of the white cotton border and attach to the back of the frame. Ensure the image faces outward from the aperture.

★ Cut a piece of the red card ¾ inch/2 cm less in length and width than the frame. Use to back the frame, securing it with double-sided tape. Glue a picture hook to the back, 2½ inches/6 cm from the top.

Festive *Napkin Holders*

These decorative napkin holders can be tailored to your color theme by selecting ribbons and beads to coordinate. Try different beads, such as those with letters for a personal touch.

MATERIALS

* craft wire—thick ($\frac{1}{16}$ inch/2 mm) and thin
* ready-made solid napkin ring
* beige thick cotton fabric
* sewing needle and beige strong cotton thread
* beads of your choice
* ribbons to match or coordinate with the beads and fabric
* white Velcro™
* scissors, tack lifter, tape measure, tailor's chalk, strong double-sided tape, extra-strong iron-on hemming tape, steam iron

* Lay the thick craft wire across the width of the napkin ring, then bend it at a right angle around the ring until it is about $1\frac{3}{8}$ inches/3.5 cm away from the right-angled bend. Bend the wire at a right angle across the ring, then again at a right angle around the other side of the ring in the other direction until you reach the beginning of the wire. Cut the wire, leaving enough surplus to twist the ends together with the tack lifter. Repeat for the number of napkin holders you require.

* Measure the width and length of one of the napkin holders and add $\frac{5}{8}$ inch/1.5 cm to each measurement. Cut two pieces of beige fabric this size for each napkin holder. On one of each pair of fabric pieces, use tailor's chalk to mark the measurements of the napkin holder, centered. Pierce through the fabric at each corner with a needle so that you can see its position on the other side.

* On the needle-pricked side of the fabric, place double-sided tape along both lengths and widths, flush to the edges. Trim the corners for a neat finish. Align a napkin holder with the pricked holes at one end. Remove the tape backing and fold the fabric edges over the wire to secure. You can sew along all the edges for extra security.

* Using the iron-on hemming tape and following the manufacturer's directions, hem the edges of the second piece of fabric so that it is $\frac{1}{4}$ inch/5 mm smaller all around than the napkin holder.

* Thread your chosen beads onto a length of the thin wire, then wrap around the napkin holder. Pierce the ends through the fabric and fold over firmly to ensure that the beads are held securely and the wire doesn't protrude. Wrap the ribbon around, securing it at the back with double-sided tape for easy removal.

* Back the napkin holder with the second hemmed piece of fabric, using thin strips of Velcro™ for easy removal.

TIP

* Alternatively, you can sew the beads and ribbon onto the napkin holder fabric for a permanent result. Sponge clean the fabric only.

Truffle *Tree*

Treat your family or friends to some luxurious nibbles presented in the form of this elegant, silk-clad tree. You can adapt the colors and use alternative edible treats, if you wish.

MATERIALS

* bamboo cane
* ceramic/terracotta plant pot about 4¼ inches/11 cm in diameter (or no less than the diameter of the polystyrene ball, below), tapering at the bottom to about 3¼ inches/8 cm in diameter
* polystyrene ball 4 inches/ 10 cm in diameter
* gold spray paint
* floristry foam
* sheet wadding
* black Velcro™
* dark ruby raw-silk fabric
* extra-strong iron-on hemming tape
* nuts and dried fruit
* gold tissue paper
* box of toothpicks
* about 60 truffles
* tape measure, pencil, mini hacksaw, old newspaper, face mask and protective gloves, strong double-sided tape, scissors, steam iron, compass with blade head attached for cutting circles, cutting mat

✷ Use the hacksaw with care to saw a piece of bamboo cane equal in length to the height of your pot, plus half the diameter of the ball and 5 inches/13 cm for the visible trunk. Mark 2 inches/5 cm along the cane and insert into the ball up to this mark. Center the ball on the cane.

✷ Lay old newspaper down in a ventilated area. Wearing a face mask and protective gloves, spray the bamboo and ball with gold paint. Let dry. Spray the rim of the pot and inside. Let dry.

✷ Firmly wedge a layer of floristry foam 2¾ inches/7 cm deep in the bottom of the pot. Gently stretch and wrap two layers of wadding around the pot, securing it with double-sided tape. Adhere one layer of the Velcro™ to the pot rim and wadding, setting aside the other layer.

✷ Cut a piece of the silk fabric large enough to fit around your pot's widest circumference, plus 1¼ inches/3 cm, and twice the height of your pot, plus ¾ inch/ 2 cm. Fold lengthwise to match the height of your pot, with the extra ¾ inch/2 cm on one side, and iron a sharp crease.

✷ Using the iron-on hemming tape and following the manufacturer's directions, fold the extra ¾ inch/2 cm over the other fabric edge and seal it to the fabric. Fold over ¾ inch/2 cm along one end of the fabric panel, onto the same side as the previous hem, and seal in the same way. Attach the other layer of Velcro™ along the top (folded) edge of the fabric panel, stopping ½ inch/1 cm short of the hemmed end. Fasten the fabric panel to the rim pot, overlapping the hemmed end and securing the overlap with double-sided tape.

✷ Insert the bamboo trunk into the center of the floristry foam. Fill the pot to the brim with nuts and dried fruit.

✷ Using the bladed compass, cut about 60 disks 2 inches/5 cm in diameter from the gold tissue paper. Break a toothpick in half and use the pointed end to pierce the polystyrene ball at the top center and push the toopthpick about halfway in. Remove and insert the pointed end into the center of a gold disk, then push it halfway into a truffle. Insert the other end into the hole in the ball. Repeat until the surface is covered.

Reindeer Tealight *Box*

This reindeer-adorned light box, illuminated by the soft glow of tealights, will add atmosphere to any area of your home. Try the mantel, dining table, or a stairwell.

MATERIALS

* 300 gsm Bockingford (slightly textured) paper
* thick tracing paper
* board 1/16 inch/2 mm thick
* clear glass tealight holders
* tealights
* scissors, painter's tape, art knife, steel rule, cutting mat, bone folder or scoring tool, strong double-sided tape

★ Enlarge the box templates on page 219 on a photocopier as directed and cut out using scissors. You may need to make the template in two halves.

★ Place the light box template over the Bockingford paper on a cutting mat and secure both with painter's tape. Using the art knife, cut out as many of the reindeer shapes as you want, depending on how many sides will be visible.

★ Cut out the light box, marking the position of the folds by piercing through to the paper at each end of the fold lines as you cut around. Remove the template. Align the ruler with the puncture marks and score along the lines with a bone folder or scoring tool.

★ Cut the tracing paper to the size of the panels from which you have cut motifs. Secure to the panels with double-sided tape along the top and bottom edges.

★ Construct the box, using double-sided tape to adhere the hem inside at the top of the box, for extra rigidity, and the side seam. Fold up the bottom of the box—it should look like the back of an envelope—using a few strips of double-sided tape in different directions to secure it.

★ Using the rectangular template, cut the platform from the board, then slot into the base of the light box. Place the tealights in clear glass tealight holders no less than 2½ inches/6 cm high and position centrally within the box. Use no more than 2 tealights per box.

WARNINGS

★ Never leave lit candles unattended.
★ Do not make this light box smaller than directed.
★ Do not place tealights inside the light box without glass holders.
★ Do not lift the box when the tealights are lit without supporting it underneath.

Advent *Calendar*

Every child knows that when the Advent calendar is hung, Christmas isn't too far away. Build the excitement by choosing your own treats and sentiments to fill this delightful calendar.

MATERIALS

* beige thick cotton fabric 39 inches/1 meter square
* red and dark-green felt
* roll of matte laminate
* 2 pieces of bamboo cane 14¼ inches/36 cm in length
* bright-red soft thick fabric 25 x 37 inches/62 x 93 cm
* sewing needle and deep-red strong cotton thread
* extra-strong iron-on hemming tape
* 6 pairs of deep-red baby socks, age 0–3 months
* 6 pairs of deep-green baby socks, age 0–3 months
* 25 Christmas-tree embellishments in red, green, and gold
* 24 tiny wooden pegs
* 59 inches/1.5-meters of ½-inch/1-cm wide green ribbon
* large silver bell
* 14¼-inch/36-cm length of ¼-inch/5-mm wide red ribbon
* art knife, steel rule, pinking shears, basting pins, basting thread, strong double-sided tape, scissors, steam iron, fabric glue

✦ Enlarge the box templates on page 219 on a photocopier as directed and cut out using scissors. Cut 24 squares from the beige fabric using an art knife and a steel ruler on a cutting mat. Cut 24 squares from red felt with pinking shears.

✦ Using the template, cut the tree from green felt, place on the beige fabric, and cut out a slightly larger tree for a border.

✦ Laminate the sheet of numbers, then cut out with the art knife and rule.

✦ Place one length of bamboo at the top of the large piece of red fabric and fold the top edge of the fabric over. Pin, then baste the hem. Hand sew with red thread, then remove the basting stitches. Repeat at the bottom of the fabric.

✦ Temporarily position all the beige squares and the beige tree on the red fabric with double-sided tape, ensuring that they are evenly positioned. Using the iron-on hemming tape around the edges and following the manufacturer's directions, adhere them to the red fabric one row at a time.

✦ Using fabric glue, adhere the red felt squares about halfway up and ¼ inch/5 mm in from the right-hand side. Use double-sided tape to adhere the numbers centrally to each red square. Adhere the green felt tree to the beige tree with fabric glue. Sew the socks to the top corners of the beige squares. Open them fully to add your treats, then stick the heels down with fabric glue. Use fabric glue to adhere the tree embellishments, ensuring sock number 24 has 2 slightly overlapping trees. Add the pegs to look like they are holding the socks up. Tie bows in the green ribbon and attach the bell, then sew to the tree in the bottom right-hand corner.

✦ To create hanging loops, use the art knife to make horizontal incisions just below the bamboo, wide enough to thread the red ribbon through and under the bamboo. Slightly overlap the ribbon and sew together. Move the ribbon around to hide the sewn part behind the bamboo. Repeat at the opposite end.

Star Tree *Topper*

Create this stunning tree topper and watch it shimmer as the light catches it at various angles. You could make matching "baubles" by simply reducing the size, eliminating the spiral, and adding a loop for hanging.

MATERIALS

- craft wire—thick (about 1/16 inch/2 mm) and thin
- silver thin shimmering thread
- silver beads and cotton thread
- 5 glass crystal beads
- scissors, art knife, cutting mat, tack lifter, gel superglue

✷ Enlarge the template on page 221 on a photocopier as directed and cut out with scissors.

✷ Using the tack lifter, bend a length of the thick wire into the star template shape, starting from the center at the bottom.

✷ When you reach your starting point, bend the metal vertically down from the base of the star and begin to create a spiral about 2½ inches/6 cm in length with 7 coils, making it wider at the bottom (about 2 inches/5 cm in diameter)—this is where the top of the tree will feed through it to secure the star.

✷ Close the gap between where you began the star and where the wire was bent vertically down by slightly overlapping the wire and criss-crossing the thin wire around the wire to bind.

✷ Tie the silver thread securely to this point and weave it around the star to create a web. Thread silver beads onto the cotton thread (about 20 inches/50 cm in length) and coil around the stem and up onto the web, forming a squiggle by gently weaving in and out. Secure in place with tiny droplets of gel superglue.

✷ Thread each crystal bead onto a small loop of wire to attach to the five points of the star.

TIP

✷ Thread some extra crystal beads onto thin wire and weave around the top of the tree and the spiral to enhance the effect.

Templates

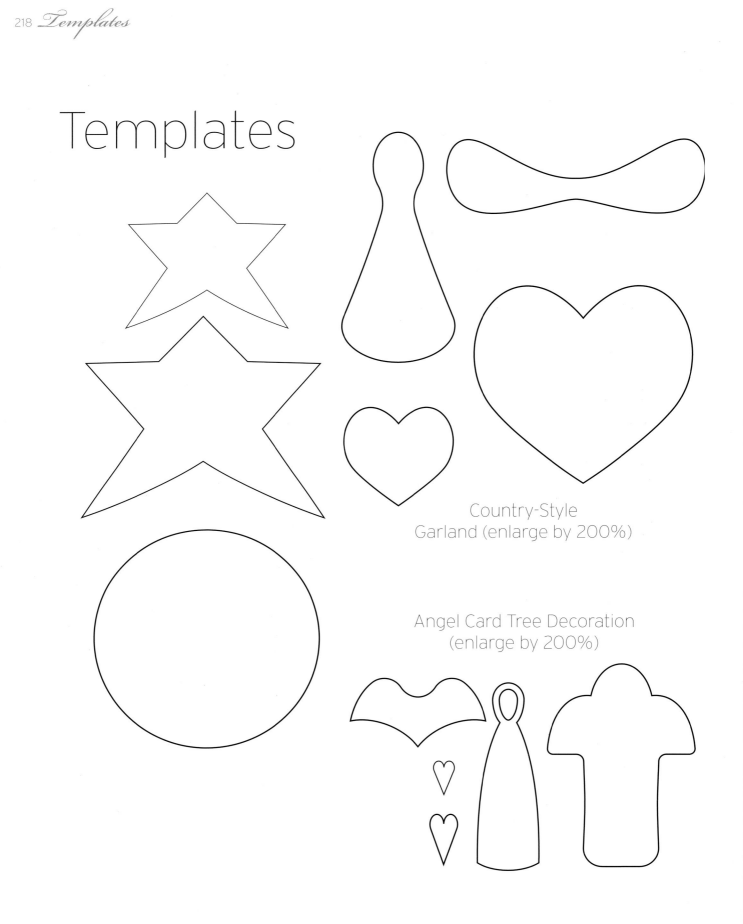

Country-Style
Garland (enlarge by 200%)

Angel Card Tree Decoration
(enlarge by 200%)

Advent Calendar
(enlarge by 200%)

1	2	3	4
5	6	7	8
9	10	11	12
13	14	15	16
17	18	19	20
21	22	23	24

Reindeer Tealight Box (enlarge by 400%)

Festive Mobile (enlarge by 200%, cross stitch pattern for visual reference only)

Christmas Snowflake Card and Snowflake Gift Box (enlarge by 200%)

Christmas Card Tree Decoration (enlarge by 200%)

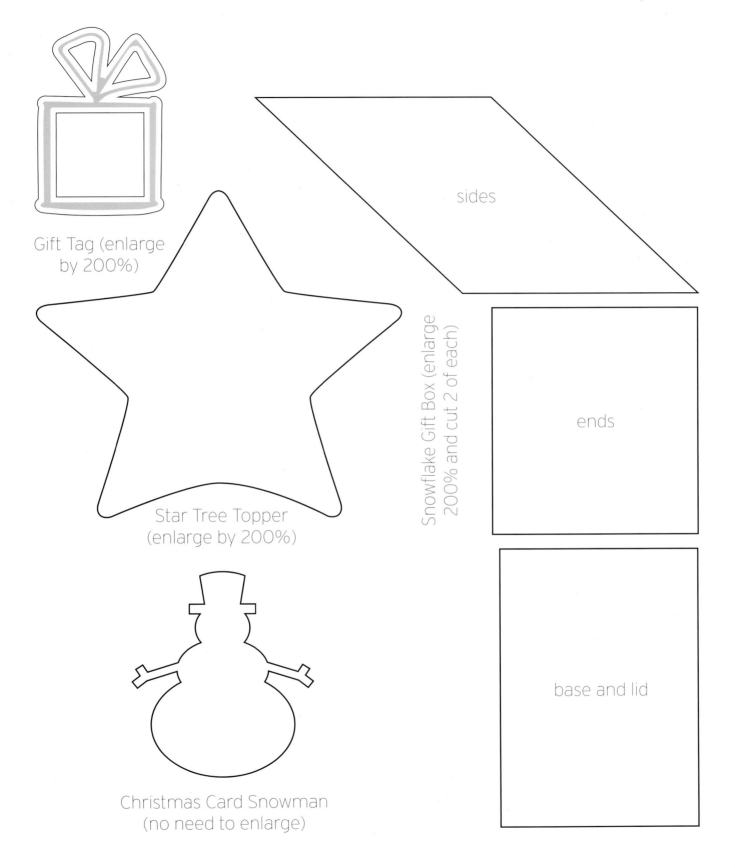

Gift Tag (enlarge
by 200%)

Star Tree Topper
(enlarge by 200%)

Christmas Card Snowman
(no need to enlarge)

sides

Snowflake Gift Box (enlarge
200% and cut 2 of each)

ends

base and lid

Index